KT-482-984

"If you are a coward like me when it comes to conflict, then this book could be perfect for you. I now appreciate the need for conflict, and I am getting even better dealing with it."
—Ken Blanchard, Coauthor,
The One Minute Manager and *Whale Done!*

"After 50 years in the service business with over 1,000 associates, I've seen and heard lots of 'experts' on people management, development, etc. Tim Ursiny is the best I know because he deals with the 'heart' of the matter, not just the apparent facts. Tim cares and he helps teach others to care. I highly recommend this book."
—Robert J. Williams, Chairman/CEO, Allied Williams Companies, Inc.

"Through humorous stories and practical exercises, Tim Ursiny lessened the paralyzing fear I can have of conflict and helped me to see the satisfaction I feel in healthy conflict resolution. I highly recommend Dr. Ursiny and *The Coward's Guide to Conflict.* It will make you laugh as it challenges you, and it will give you the tools you need to work with your difficult people."
—Randall M. Hultgren, State Representative,
Illinois General Assembly

"Dr. Ursiny's book offers hope for the meek without requiring them to become part of the problem. And the real-life examples help readers understand how to apply these principles both at home and at work."
—David Davoust, President, Robis, Inc.

"As a service-oriented company, the concepts and guidelines for dealing with conflict are invaluable not only within our workplace, but also in dealing with our clients. A must-read for anyone working in a service-based organization!"
—Stephen Johnson, CEO, Mars Hill Data Solutions, Inc.

"Dr. Ursiny provides an entertaining and refreshing viewpoint on a topic that is critical to success in business. He demonstrates that dealing effectively with conflict is not only possible, it can be relatively easy when you listen to his practical advice."
—Lanny Hoel, Assistant Vice President, Organization Development,
Trustmark Insurance Company

"Tim speaks from a wealth of personal and professional experience with an amazing understanding of people. In this book you will find yourself, you will believe that the stories and situations are illustrations from your life. And at the end, your final thought will be, 'Why didn't I think of that? Hey, I CAN DO THAT!'"
—Dave Moore, Owner, ServiceMaster Franchise

"This book is truly life-changing. The techniques are simple yet powerful. I have read and made use of many 'self-help' books in the past, but none have had the profound impact upon my life as this book has."
—Kevin Russeau, DC, DIBCN, President, Russeau Team Healthcare

"What an important book at a time of such world conflict. Dr. Tim reminds us that the antidote for dealing with conflict is connection, humanity, and courage."
—Wendy Johnson, MC, CEC, CMC, President and CEO,
National Association of Business Coaches

"Tim Ursiny's life message is a call to resolve conflict, and he speaks so directly and practically about this critical topic. Over the past decade, we have benefited tremendously from his wise counsel, penetrating insight, and great advice. Through his latest book, you will too!"
—Jeff and Lora Helton, Coauthors of *Authentic Marriages*
and *The Authentic Marriages Workbook*

"A great guide for anyone who has ever had reservations about confrontation! After reading Dr. Tim's new book, you'll find yourself saying, 'Put me in, COACH. I'm ready to play!'"
—Jimmy PS Hayes, Retail Manager

"*The Coward's Guide to Conflict* is more than a delightful read. It is a practical guide that clearly identifies the challenges that surround conflict while providing solutions that work. Dr. Ursiny's magnetic authenticity and humor lace each page, while illuminating the path for any conflict coward who dares to walk toward the challenge of change."
—Judy Santos, Life Coach, Founder & President, Christian Coaches Network

"Management students at Hamilton College greatly enhanced their people skills through *The Coward's Guide to Conflict*. Tim Ursiny shines a light of confidence and direction for managers to follow in resolving conflict. Hamilton College students now have an insight into how to effectively nurture people through the many stages of conflict."
—Craig McCoy, Management Instructor,
Hamilton College, Des Moines, Iowa

"The merit of this book lies not only in Tim's strength of analysis and trustworthy advice (such as identifying a personal conflict style), but also in simply shedding some light on inevitable conflicts before they occur, saving much of the confusion caused by charging ahead blindly."
—Steve Carlson, Life Member of MDRT

"Tim sheds light on the truth about conflict in his book, demonstrating that conflict is actually an opportunity for greater intimacy if we will only run toward the battle with courage, instead of away in cowardice."
—Kelly Brady, Family Life Pastor, Glen Ellyn Bible Church,
Glen Ellyn, Illinois

"Dr. Ursiny's book takes the fear out of dealing with challenging relationships where conflict is a major factor. This book is thoughtful and offers a practical, nonjudgmental approach to dealing with tough subjects. I'm recommending this book to my patients."
—Dr. Margaret Dempster, President,
Dempster Natural Health

"Dr. Ursiny shows us everyday people how to understand where conflict comes from, where it shows up, and how to make conscious decisions on how to deal with it. This book is a must have for everyone that is interested in conflict resolution."
—Tricia Nickel, President, Wolftec

"*The Coward's Guide to Conflict* is a helpful, informative text that provides effective ways to deal with conflict in an easily readable style...and the principles and techniques he uses are grounded in solid psychological research. I plan to include some of Dr. Ursiny's material in my learning and motivation classes."
—Ed Callen, Professor of Psychology

"Many of my clients have used Tim Ursiny's TruthTalk formula to manage conflict with their employees, colleagues, and family members. *The Coward's Guide to Conflict* is one of the best resources I found available in providing step-by-step methods to handle conflict."
—Kathi Graham-Leviss, President, XB Coaching, Inc.

"Many of the details in this book come from the author's own family and professional experience, and this is where the writing really sizzles with both relevance and humor. The book is not only a source of explanation about the value and purpose of conflict, but because of its personal focus it also provides a source for inspiration and motivation to engage in difficult conversations rather than running away."
—Rey A. Carr, Ph.D., CEO, Peer Resources

"Dr. Tim offers tremendous insight and strategy into effectively dealing with a subject that affects the quality of our relationships in every aspect of our lives—family, friends, work, community, society."
—Patrick J. Woelfel, Central Division Director, UBS PaineWebber

"*The Coward's Guide to Conflict* takes so much of the pain out of one of life's most difficult issues. It is an incredible guide for positive communication."
—Jan Madori, CEO, Personal Preference

"This book is both a field manual and reference guide, and will greatly benefit anyone seeking to be a more effective communicator. Anyone who deals with conflict should refer to it often."
—Todd Martin, Chairman, Global Security International

"Those of us in education are in a unique position when it comes to the influence we have on those in the next generation, either in direct conflict with them and/or modeling appropriate behavior. Chronic avoiders, such as myself, will find Dr. Ursiny's insights invaluable."
—David Smith, High School Teacher/Coach, Glenbrook South High School

"A useful, practical, and inspiring guide and workbook for setting your moral compass and pursuing a path to deal with common conflicts and challenges."
—Dan Jana, Founder, Great Teleseminars.com, PR LEADS.com, and ShowStoppers.com

"*The Coward's Guide to Conflict* was one of the most refreshing books that I've read in years. The techniques Tim suggests are both honest and simple. A great resource for anyone who is or who knows a conflict coward."
—Joreen Redeker, Homemaker; Family Conflict Manager

The *coward's* guide to conflict

The
coward's
guide to
conflict

Empowering Solutions for
Those Who Would
Rather Run Than Fight

TIM URSINY, Ph.D.

SOURCEBOOKS, INC.®
NAPERVILLE, ILLINOIS

Copyright © 2003 by Timothy E. Ursiny
Cover and internal design © 2003 by Sourcebooks, Inc.
Cover images © Kramer Photographers

All rights reserved. No part of this book may be reproduced in any form or by any electronic or mechanical means including information storage and retrieval systems—except in the case of brief quotations embodied in critical articles or reviews—without permission in writing from its publisher, Sourcebooks, Inc.

This publication is designed to provide accurate and authoritative information in regard to the subject matter covered. It is sold with the understanding that the publisher is not engaged in rendering legal, accounting, or other professional service. If legal advice or other expert assistance is required, the services of a competent professional person should be sought.—*From a Declaration of Principles Jointly Adopted by a Committee of the American Bar Association and a Committee of Publishers and Associations*

Published by Sourcebooks, Inc.
P.O. Box 4410, Naperville, Illinois 60567-4410
(630) 961-3900
FAX: (630) 961-2168
www.sourcebooks.com

Library of Congress Cataloging-in-Publication Data

Ursiny, Timothy E.
  The coward's guide to conflict : Empowering solutions for those who would rather run than fight / by Timothy E. Ursiny.
      p. cm.
  Includes bibliographical references and index.
  ISBN 1-4022-0055-2 (pbk. : alk. paper)
  1. Interpersonal conflict. 2. Conflict management. I. Title.
BF637.I48 U76 2003
303.6—dc21

                                                2002153631

Printed and bound in the United States of America
VHG 10 9 8 7 6 5 4 3 2 1

Dedication

In memory of my father, Kenneth Richard Ursiny. I wish that you were around to see this. Thank you for encouraging me to speak before audiences and for the friendship we developed as I grew older.

In memory of my grandmother, Imogene "Nanny" Vance. You were always so good to everyone around you. I wish more people in this world could be like you.

Table of Contents

Introduction   xvii

Section I: You're Not the Only One Out There Who Hates Conflict   1

    Chapter 1: Take the Coward Test   3

    Chapter 2: Seven Choices You Can Make In Conflict   13

    Chapter 3: The Top Ten Reasons People Avoid Conflict   25

    Chapter 4: Why Change?   35

Section II: How to Motivate Yourself to Deal with Conflict   43

    Chapter 5: The Secret for Making Yourself Face Conflict   45

    Chapter 6: Confronting Your Fear One Step at a Time   57

    Chapter 7: How to Make Conflict Less Frightening...Quickly   63

    Chapter 8: How Your Integrity Can Help You Face Conflict   69

    Chapter 9: Understanding When Conflict Is Actually a Good Thing   75

    Chapter 10: Building Your Knowledge, Skills, and Confidence   83

Section III: Common Causes of Conflict   87

    Chapter 11: We'd Be Fine if *They* Weren't So Different!   89

    Chapter 12: Why People Only Think That They're Angry   105
          (Often They're Not!)

    Chapter 13: Five Ways to Listen and Why People Don't Use Them   113

    Chapter 14: Four Communication Patterns to Use if You   125
          Want to Keep Fighting

    Chapter 15: Don't Assume the Position   135

Chapter 16: The Role of Selfishness 145

Chapter 17: If Common Sense Is So Common, Then Why Don't 155
They Have It?

Section IV: You've Got the Tools, You've Got the Talent: 167
Techniques to Handle Any Conflict

Chapter 18: The Truth and Nothing But the Truth: Using TruthTalk 169

Chapter 19: The Relationship between Wants, Fairness, and Integrity 189

Chapter 20: Assertiveness, Coward Style 201

Chapter 21: Avoiding the Top Ten Mistakes Made When Dealing 213
with Upset People

Chapter 22: Talking About How You Are Talking 227

Chapter 23: The Lesson of the Swaying Trees: Embracing Conflict 239

Chapter 24: Putting It All Together: A Step-by-Step Approach 249
for Dealing with Conflict

Conclusion: Is It Worth It and Can I Still Be a Coward? 263

Appendix 267

Bibliography 275

Index 277

Acknowledgments

A big thank you to the team at Sourcebooks and to Dominique Raccah for being a publisher who truly cares about impacting the world. She has the heart, strength, and vision that any writer would yearn for from his publisher. For my editor, Jennifer Fusco, who has a gentle and encouraging spirit combined with incredible ability and professionalism. For Megan Dempster, who created a great cover design. Also, a big thanks to Judith Kelly, Maggy Tinucci, and Andy Sachs, and all of the publicity department for the support that they have given me that has already gone beyond my expectations. I thank you all for how you combine heart and quality with a love for books and what they can do for our world.

This book would not have been possible without the clients that I have had over the years. Your genuiness in sharing your stories has enriched my life. You are the best part of my work. You make it all worthwhile, fun, and meaningful. Thank you for sharing both your laughter and your tears.

My thanks to the extraordinary people at Personal Preference. You beautify homes with art, but you also beautify lives with your commitment to relationships. The work that we have done over the years has honed my skills and warmed my heart. I usually tested out my stories on you before putting them in the book. Your laughter and engagement guided me well. And special thanks to Jan Madori who has created a company that truly impacts people's lives for the positive. Jan, you are a dear friend and an inspiration to me. You have supported my work every step of the way. Words cannot capture how grateful I am for all that you have done.

I also want to thank all of the coaches and staff at Advantage Coaching & Training for their steadfast support and encouragement in this project. All of you have been so great through all of this. We all deserve to celebrate this accomplishment together.

The friends that have given me encouragement in this project are too numerous to mention. You know who you are and I thank you from the bottom of my heart. However, a special thanks to Steve Johnson. Years ago, Steve encouraged me to start a little consulting practice on the side while I was trying to figure out what to do with my life. Obviously, this "little consulting practice" has turned into a life's work and passion. Steve, you are a man of wisdom and you are always there for me. I appreciate it more than you know.

I would also like to thank my mother, Frances Knight, for instilling a loving heart in her son. Mom, your gentle spirit has always been a good model for me. Thank you for always teaching me that I could do great things.

None of this would mean a thing to me without the care and support of my family. My wife, Marla, has supported this dream for years, and continues to amaze me with her unconditional love, forgiveness, and random acts of kindness. Thanks, honey, for building intimacy by going through conflict and for continuing to build our lives together. Your love is my sanctuary. My sons bring light to my life. Zach, Colton, and Vance, you guys are the best. Thanks for playing with me even when I get home later than I said I would. You warm my heart when you all cry out "Daddy" when I walk through the door.

And God, I thank You as always for grace and blessings beyond what I deserve.

Introduction

I hate conflict! I really do. Not just a little, but a lot. I hated it growing up, I hated it when I got married, and I hate it now that I'm a psychologist and executive coach and corporate trainer. To me, there was never a need for conflict. We should all just hold hands and sing "We Are the World" and everything would be OK. So, despite all of my training, I have never grown to like conflict. However, I have grown to be very capable of dealing with it. I've also grown to believe that conflict is actually (gasp) good at times. While I don't love it, I can appreciate the need for it and the actual benefits that can come from healthy disagreements.

If you picked up this book then you are probably someone like me. You hate it when someone is upset with you. You quickly tense up when someone raises his or her voice. You watch the news and just shake your head in disbelief at all of the hurt and anger in the world. Unfortunately, you and I can throw a thousand coins in a thousand wishing wells and we still cannot take conflict out of this world. So we can run, but we cannot hide! We can sprint, jog, scream, deny, avoid, and make any other desperate attempt to get away from conflict, but we cannot make conflict disappear from our lives. Conflict is a part of life. And, like it or not, you will have to deal with it in some way.

In my professional life I come across conflict all the time. For seven years I was a psychologist in private practice. During that time I learned just how lousy people were at dealing with conflict, especially married couples. However, I always assumed that my perceptions of how well people managed conflict were skewed. Perhaps my clients did not represent the norm. They were people who were having problems, so logically they would be worse than the average person in terms of dealing with conflict. Right? Good theory, but I could not have been more wrong. In 1997 I started Advantage Coaching & Training, Inc. and transitioned to being a personal and executive coach and trainer. In my coaching and training work I help people defeat blocks to their success and live more fulfilling lives. I basically act as a personal trainer for the mind. I help people bring out their best skills, attitudes, and actions so that they live conscious lives. I have dealt with individuals of all sorts—small business owners, CEOs of mid-sized companies, executives at Fortune 100 companies, just about all types of individuals—and guess what? Most people are lousy at handling conflict. I don't care if you are a senior executive, a CEO, a maintenance engineer, or a home-schooling parent, human beings on the whole have a lot to learn when it comes to handling conflict.

However, I have found that the individuals who achieve unusual levels of success in life do have some common beliefs and behaviors concerning conflict. Most people who are truly successful have built an incredible team or community around themselves. This act alone requires them to know how to handle conflict. Truly successful people just seem to know something about how to relate to and motivate other people. They are able to work through conflicts in order to build more loyal and solid relationships. Successful people know how to resolve conflict. But here is one secret that may surprise you. Despite their level of success, despite their position in their community or in life, despite their vast wisdom, most successful people still hate conflict. Just like most people, they dislike the tension that conflict produces. However, unlike many people, they know what to do about it.

So, what do most people think about conflict?

When I do workshops on conflict in corporations, I routinely ask, "What words and feelings come up for you when you think about conflict?" Here are some common responses:

- Fear
- Loss
- Humiliation
- Run
- Loss of productivity

- Hurt
- Bad
- Terror
- Anger
- Pain

Do you notice anything about the above list? They are all negative words. Usually, all I get from the audience is a list of negative words. When we think of conflict, we think of something bad. But what is conflict? When we use the word conflict in this book, we merely will be referring to differences in perspective, beliefs, actions, or interests. Sometimes these differences are verbalized and sometimes they are not, but either way conflict exists.

Despite the fact that many of us see conflict as something negative and are lousy at handling it, the exciting thing is that *there are some great ways* to deal with conflict. And you can achieve fantastic results from dealing with conflict well. Some examples of great results from dealing with conflict are:

- Better relationships
- Increased confidence
- Less anger and depression
- Greater respect from others
- Greater self-respect
- Increased intimacy
- Career enhancement (such as raises, promotions, easier days, etc.)
- Peace
- Less fear
- Greater sense of personal strength

Perhaps you know that it would be better to deal with conflict, but you wonder...

- How can I get myself to deal with conflict when I'm too afraid?
- If I decide to deal with a conflict, how do I do it?
- How can I handle someone who is upset without making her more upset?
- How do I confront someone without hurting his feelings?
- How can I deal with conflict with my boss or coworker without getting fired?

This book will give you answers for all of the above. This is a book for people who hate conflict. Therefore, we will look at conflict through the eyes of a conflict-avoider. The book is divided into four sections.

Section I: You're Not the Only One Out There Who Hates Conflict

Section II: How to Motivate Yourself to Deal with Conflict

Section III: Common Causes of Conflict

Section IV: You've Got the Tools, You've Got the Talent: Techniques to Handle Any Conflict

Chapter 24 brings together all of the tools that we will explore throughout the book and combines them into a step-by-step approach for dealing with conflict. Finally, we will conclude with "Is It Worth It and Can I Still Be a Coward?" as a wrap-up to our journey and a reminder that you need to be true to yourself and your personality as you consider this new path.

Within each chapter, I have created a structural skeleton to follow. Each chapter will follow the same basic structure and flow:

Real life: Contains a story that has applications to conflict. Client stories will be disguised and will combine characteristics from several of my clients in order to respect the individual's confidentiality. Some examples will be work examples and some will be from home (given that most principles apply in both places).

How it applies: Expands on the principles related in the real life story. This section will explain how the stories relate to our lives and explore principles for dealing with conflict.

Exercises: Contains questions and/or activities to help you coach yourself in dealing with conflict. I highly recommend that you do these! Do not just read them and go on to the next chapter. You will get the most out of this book by doing the exercises.

Next steps and additional resources: Provides suggestions on how to make the principles and exercises real to your life as well as additional resources for exploring the chapter topic. Each chapter will end with a quote or two related to the chapter content said in words better than mine.

From one conflict hater to another, let me tell you that I admire your courage for picking up this book. I trust that you will grow as you take this journey to change your relationship with conflict. I have taken this journey myself and the results are worth the effort!

You're Not the Only One Out There Who Hates Conflict

Chapter 1

Take the Coward Test

Some people thrive on conflict. If you do, then put down this book and go pick up something in the next aisle of the bookstore like *How to Make Friends and Influence People*. This book is for people who dislike conflict. Some of these conflict cowards walk slowly away from conflict and others run for the hills. They do not pass go, they do not collect their $200, they go right past the conflict and end up in the jail of suppressed feelings and powerlessness. Are you a conflict coward? If you are, relax, you are definitely not alone. In this chapter you can discover just how much of a conflict coward you really are.

Real life

With each of the following real examples, rate how much of a conflict coward the person was using the following scale:

How afraid was this person of facing the conflict?

1	2	3	4	5
Not at all	Mildly	Some	Significantly	Totally

Example #1: I really should fire him, but...

Jason ran a successful computer consulting firm. He had built the firm from scratch and was at the point of having more than forty-five employees when he called me up for some coaching sessions. One of Jason's dilemmas was that he had the tendency to hire friends and friends of friends in his business.

Therefore, he struggled with his identity with his employees. Was he a friend or was he a boss? Sometimes these roles could match and sometimes they were in direct contrast to each other. One of Jason's employees, Chris, was a particular challenge.

Chris had been an old college buddy who was good for a laugh and a fun time, but not a particularly disciplined individual. Chris tended to come in late, leave early, and on many days, Jason had no clue what Chris was actually doing. I asked Jason how Chris responded when Jason confronted this behavior. With slight embarrassment, Jason hemmed and hawed in response to the question, and finally admitted, "I have never come out and directly told Chris that I am upset with what he is doing. But I shouldn't have to! He should just be more responsible." I asked Jason how long he had been upset with Chris's behavior. He stated, "This has been going on for over a year. I am furious with him, but I hate firing people." I asked, "How many people have you fired?" to which Jason sheepishly looked up at me and said, "None."

How afraid was Jason of facing the conflict?

1	2	3	4	5
Not at all	Mildly	Some	Significantly	Totally

Example #2: That's OK. I'll take care of it.

Mary was the director of the nursery at her church. It was a large church with many young families. Because of the number of children in the congregation, Mary depended on volunteers to help with child care during the services. The previous director had implemented a rule that if one of the volunteers needed to cancel within twenty-four hours of the service, he or she would be responsible for finding a replacement. Otherwise, this last-minute responsibility would fall to the director who was already working hard to fill the spots each week. The previous director was firm about this and was able to keep this boundary. Mary, however, was a pushover.

Mary's phone would often ring the night before the church service, and the conversations sounded like this:

Volunteer: Hi, Mary, it's Sue. Say, I won't be able to work in the nursery tomorrow because my sister is coming into town and we are planning to head into the city for the day.

Mary: Oh, were you able to find someone to replace you?

Volunteer: You know, I just didn't think about it until tonight. So I haven't had the chance to call anyone. I'm not sure who I could call, but I thought that you could handle it.

Mary: (Silence) Well, OK, I'm sure I can find someone, even though it is pretty late.

Volunteer: I just haven't seen my sister in awhile and I thought that it would be fun to go downtown with her. You know how it is with sisters.

Mary: Sure, don't you worry, it's OK. I'll get on the phone right now. You two have a good time. Bye.

Mary's husband (who overheard the conversation): What was that all about?

Mary: I can't believe people are so irresponsible!

How afraid was Mary of facing the conflict?

1	2	3	4	5
Not at all	Mildly	Some	Significantly	Totally

Example #3: I just can't work with you anymore.

Jan and David worked in different departments of a large corporation and had recently started a friendship. Each of them confided in the other some of their work-related fears. David feared that his abilities were not recognized by others and was concerned that he would be overlooked for a promotion if he was not able to market himself better within the corporation. Most of his accomplishments were low-visibility, and he needed to have a public "win." Jan's fears were more about personal relationships with her peers. She had a history of feeling rejected by others and was starting to feel some similar patterns with her current peers. One day a special project was announced that would require the combined effort of both of their departments. Their managers asked for volunteers to join the project team.

Before the fourth meeting of this team, David's department was responsible for writing up a strategy and opportunities analysis. David was prominently featured in this analysis, and saw this as a great opportunity for improving his visibility with the group. Once the meeting started, several people made comments about the analysis. It was a mixture of positive and negative, but it did not feel critical to David. However, when it was Jan's turn to comment, she said, "I found it completely unreadable. It was done so badly I just threw it in the trash." The room grew silent. David was shocked. He knew that Jan tended to be blunt, but she knew how important this was for him. How could she be so insensitive?

David retorted, "Well Jan, that seems unfair of you to dismiss the whole report like that." With his comment, several other members of the team agreed and were somewhat critical of Jan's comments. After this discussion, the meeting ended.

David emailed Jan later that day to ask her what had happened in that meeting. Jan replied that their friendship was over because she could not be in a relationship with someone who would set her up like that. She felt like David had betrayed her by "turning the group against her." She no longer wanted to have any contact with him. David was flabbergasted. "Isn't she the one who hurt me?" he wondered. However, in order to make peace with Jan he wrote an email apologizing for his behavior and for the fact that he had hurt her feelings. Jan simply wrote back that she could not work with someone of such low integrity, and that she did not want to discuss it further.

The next day David resigned from the team with no explanation to his peers except that his schedule had gotten very busy.

How afraid was Jan of facing the conflict?

1	2	3	4	5
Not at all	Mildly	Some	Significantly	Totally

How afraid was David of facing the conflict?

1	2	3	4	5
Not at all	Mildly	Some	Significantly	Totally

How it applies

All of the examples above should be rated 4 or 5. In the first example, Jason had taken no steps to deal with the situation. He was completely avoiding the confrontation. In example #2, Mary put up some very mild passive resistance at first, but eventually allowed the person calling to avoid taking any responsibility. She actually gave Sue permission to back out of her responsibility, despite her criticism when talking to her husband after the call. In example #3, Jan showed no ability to deal with the conflict. She merely vented on David, made hurtful accusations, and then removed herself from the experience. David initially confronted her behavior in the group (which may have been a poor choice given her sensitivities), but apologized even when he felt like he was the one who was wronged. He then dropped out of the team in order to avoid the awkwardness of the situation. In all of the examples, the avoidance had negative consequences for each individual. In example #1, Jason suffered with internal frustration, and Chris was cheated out of a confrontation that could help make him a better worker. In example #2, Mary suffered because she was reinforcing irresponsibility in her volunteers, the volunteer was cheated out of a potential growth experience in responsibility, and Mary's husband had to listen to Mary complain the rest of the night about irresponsible people. In example #3, both Jan and David had their worst fears come true and lost a friendship. Avoiding conflict can have huge costs.

Believe it or not, the vast majority of people you meet hate conflict. They run from it, they hide from it, they even pretend it doesn't exist. There are more conflict cowards out there than there are people who like conflict. That's the good news; you are not alone. Unfortunately, that is the bad news, too. We are frightened of conflict, and avoiding conflict usually ends up in even more destruction, conflict, and pain. So, how frightened of conflict are you? Do you just have a mild aversion to it or are you a full-blown conflict coward (like I was for most of my life)? Here is a test to help you answer that question.

How frightened of conflict are you?

Assign each of the statements below a number between 1 and 5:

    1= I never act or feel this way. Why did I even buy this book? I love conflict!

    2= I act or feel this way on rare occasions.

    3= I sometimes act or feel this way.

    4= I often feel or act this way.

    5= You got me. Fits me to a tee.

I hold in my real feelings when I am upset with someone because I don't want to hurt him.

                              Your rating: _____

I rarely disagree with my boss (if you don't currently have a boss, answer this question for the last time you did have a boss).

                              Your rating: _____

I rarely disagree with my friends or significant other.

                              Your rating: _____

It is easier for me to ignore it when someone upsets me than to tell them what I feel.

                              Your rating: _____

When someone raises his or her voice, I get all tense inside and just want to escape.

                              Your rating: _____

People walk all over me.

Your rating: _____

I hate going back to stores to return something even if there is something wrong with it.

Your rating: _____

I would rather work through my anger myself than to resolve it with the person who upset me.

Your rating: _____

I have a long fuse, but when I blow, I really blow!

Your rating: _____

I never blow up, but I often feel depressed and sad.

Your rating: _____

Friends say that I am passive or that I should stand up for myself more.

Your rating: _____

When I get really mad at someone, I start avoiding her.

Your rating: _____

I have ended relationships without trying to talk through our differences.

Your rating: _____

I often hold my opinion to myself when I think that someone will disagree.

Your rating: _____

I think that it is terrible to disagree with others.

Your rating: _____

I have lent money or things to people and wanted them back, but was afraid to ask.

Your rating: _____

I have quit a job because I didn't want to work with a coworker anymore (without trying to fix the problem).

Your rating: _____

I say that I am sorry to end an argument even when I think that I did not do anything wrong.

Your rating: _____

I secretly think that I am right, but don't often say it.

Your rating: _____

When I have an argument with someone, I can't stop thinking about it until we resolve it.

Your rating: _____

I am afraid to get into an argument because I might say the wrong thing.

Your rating: _____

Now, add up all of your ratings. The lowest number possible is 21 and the highest possible is 105.

Your total: _____

How did you do? Use the following scale to determine just how much of a conflict coward you are:

21–40 = What? Did you buy this book for a friend? Go give it to him!

41–60 = Not bad, you can probably use a little "tweaking" in how you deal with conflict.

61–80 = You have made a good investment in this book. Follow the principles and your life will be easier.

81–105 = Like you needed a test to figure this out! Study this book daily in order to become a lean, mean, conflict-facing machine!

Seriously, and all tests aside, it is completely up to you to determine how fearful you are of conflict and what you want to do about it. I trust that you will know how much to invest in reading, studying, and utilizing the principles of this book. I do promise you, however, that if you study this book, do the exercises, and follow the principles, you will not only make your life better, but you may actually end up improving the lives of people around you. Welcome to the journey, and remember, you are not alone!

Exercises

Self-examination exercise: The impact on your life

Take the time to examine how being a conflict coward has impacted your life. Write three to four examples below about the negative impact that avoiding conflict has created for you. Refer back to this section if your motivation to change ever diminishes.

Self-examination exercise: The impact on the lives of those around you

Write down the names of three people in your life who would benefit if you improved your ability to face conflict in a healthy way. Note specifically how their lives would improve (i.e., "They would feel greater intimacy with me," "They would benefit from seeing some things in their life that they need to change," "They might start treating people better," etc.).

Person #1: _____

The benefit is _____

_____

Person #2: _____

The benefit is _____

_____

Person #3: _____
The benefit is _____

_____

Next steps and additional resources

Develop a schedule for working through this book. Make a commitment to reread every chapter and to do the exercises rather than skip over them. Commit to studying this material rather than skimming over it.

For additional inspiration on how to triumph over something that is difficult, try *Unstoppable: 45 Powerful Stories of Perseverance and Triumph from People Just Like You* by Cynthia Kersey.

"Any fact facing us is not as important as our attitude toward it, for that determines our success or failure."
—Norman Vincent Peale

"I am not hard—I'm frightfully soft. But I will not be hounded."
—Margaret Thatcher

Chapter 2:

Seven Choices You Can Make in Conflict

There are many choices you can make when confronted with a conflict. In this chapter we will look at seven possible choices; avoid, give in, be - passive-aggressive, bully, compromise, problem-solve, and honor. We will start with seven brief stories that illustrate each of these.

Real life

Example #1: Thank goodness for caller I.D.

Cynthia knew that the call was coming. This particular customer had been calling every morning for the past three days. The customer was irate at a service issue that was not Cynthia's fault. Unfortunately, every solution she used to please the customer had failed. The technician who had been at the customer site the previous day had warned Cynthia that the customer was planning to call and give her "a piece of his mind." So when the customer's phone number popped up on Cynthia's caller I.D., she just stared at the ringing phone. She thought that he would give up after six rings, but he didn't. "Don't you get it? I'm not here!" she barked at the phone. It took eleven rings before the customer gave up. Twenty minutes later, the phone rang again and it was his number on the caller I.D.

Example #2: It's our policy.

Tom had waited for six months to get the home theater of his dreams. He had researched all the right magazines and asked all of the right questions. Finally, he made his big purchase. In addition to buying the DVD player, the projector, his surround sound equipment, and the 120-inch roll-down screen, he also purchased fifteen DVDs in order to get started on his movie-going experience. The screen was on back order so he had to wait several weeks before it was delivered. Once the screen arrived, Tom worked feverishly to set everything up. Stepping back to admire his accomplishment, he plugged the DVD player in and was ready to make the popcorn when he noticed that the picture quality was poor. After trying several movies and testing all of the equipment, he came to the conclusion that the DVD player he had bought was defective. Despite the late hour, he grabbed the player and hopped in his car to drive to the store. He had waited six months for this moment and he did not want to wait a moment more.

When Tom explained the problem to the person at the return desk, she told to him that they would have to send the DVD player in for repairs and that it would take at least three weeks for the unit to be fixed. Tom complained and asked for a replacement machine. Unfortunately, the store had a two-week limit on returns for players, and due to Tom's waiting for his screen, he was two days over the time limit. Tom explained that he had not opened up the equipment because he was waiting for the screen, but the person at the desk just continued to say that it was store policy and that he would just have to wait to get the unit back. Tom was furious, but simply looked at the person and said, "Fine, just give me the paperwork."

Example #3: The look

My best friend Steve and I are movie buddies. There are few things we enjoy more than going to the movies, getting a huge bucket of popcorn with far too much butter and salt, and then watching an action flick with minimal plot and maximum adrenaline. However, almost every time we sit down to enjoy our movie we are plagued by the dreaded "talkers."

You know the type. They talk about anything. You get to hear how their day was, you get to hear the end of the movie if they have seen it before, you get to hear how they have an outfit at home just like the one the actress is wearing. In other words, you get to hear anything that you have absolutely zero interest in hearing. While this irritates me, it is nothing compared to what it does to Steve.

One of Steve's gifts is the art of passive-aggressive behavior. His typical response to "talkers" contains the following (in chronological order):

1) The head shake
2) The audible sigh
3) The incredulous look
4) And the finale, the dramatic move to another seat

Rarely, someone will stop talking when Steve just shakes his head in the "This can't be happening to us again" fashion. Frequently, it takes at least the full audible sigh and the "look" to get someone to quiet down. The look is powerful. It is brief enough as not to invite a retort and mainly consists of his head tilted to one side, mouth open, and eyes wide in disbelief. Usually, none of these techniques work and we have to move seats. Of course, the movement is sharp and every aspect of our bodies attempts to send guilt and shame to "the talkers." Equally true is the fact that I doubt any of them ever have had to enter therapy due to the shame we created.

Steve has become much more assertive over the years. And let me warn you, never have your cell phone on when you are in the movie theater and he is there. Trust me, it isn't pretty.

Example #4: My way or the highway

Patrick had heard about the rumblings before he officially joined the department. He was told how two talented individuals within the department did great individual work, but were constantly at each other's throat. He had just been brought into the department as part of the merger and was put in charge of supervising the two individuals. Patrick was a man used to getting his way, and he was not going to let the difficulties of these two team members interfere with his success in making the business unit more profitable. In his first week as their supervisor he pulled them into his office and said the following:

"I hear that the two of you have problems with each other. I hear that you don't work well as a team. I hear that this has gone on for some time. I want you to know this. I don't care what your problem is with each other. I don't care whose fault it was. I don't care if you never learn to like each other. But you will learn how to work together. From this point on you are to treat each other with respect. I hear anything contrary to that and it will impact your bonuses for this year. And if it doesn't get better you can both go out and find a different job because you may do good work, but you are not indispensable. This company was here before you came and this company will stay alive if you go. I will not accept conflict between my senior staff. So you two figure out what you need to do and do it." And after finishing scolding them like children, he finished with, "Now go out there and act like professionals."

Example #5: Yes, your honor, it was Mickey Mouse that broke us up.

My wife loves Disney World, but our last trip to Florida almost became just that. Marla and I are very different in the way we like to experience vacations. Marla is very methodical. She loves vacation and wants to plan well because she doesn't want to miss anything. I, on the other hand, am very spontaneous. Since I tend to be very disciplined in my work, I like vacations to be free from routine and structure. My idea of going to Disney World is to get up whenever you happen to wake up, enjoy the breakfast buffet at the hotel, and then head to the park. Once in the park, you go on whatever captures you attention. Sounds like fun, right? Well, not according to my lovely wife. Marla's idea of visiting Disney World is the following:

Step 1: Order Orlando books from AAA.

Step 2: Review information and cross-reference with other travel books.

Step 3: Interview friends who have been there recently for highlights and things to avoid.

Step 4: Start mapping out the most efficient way to experience each park, taking into consideration travel times, required bathroom breaks, and ride intensity as compared to time since last meal.

And the list goes on.

So when we get to Disney World she is a woman on a mission, she has her map, her notes, and her method.

You can imagine how well the two of us interacted the first day at the park. We both were frustrated at each other's tendencies and expectations, and started stupid discussions like, "This just symbolizes what is wrong with our marriage." In reality, the best part of our marriage is the fact that we are different and we would be lost without each other. Fortunately, we were able to resolve our dilemma by doing half the time her way (planned and methodical) and half the time my way (free and spontaneous). It turned out to be a good vacation.

Example #6: How about a raise?

The economy was tough and Jim was feeling it. He had started his company five years earlier and had a tough first year. His success significantly increased when he hired Brandon as his director of sales at the end of the first year in business. Brandon had done a marvelous job in increasing the profitability of the company. And even though the current year was challenging, Brandon was largely responsible for keeping the company afloat. The problem came when Brandon received a job offer from another company that would increase his salary by 15 percent. He had a son entering college and needed the extra income. When Brandon brought this up to Jim, it was awkward and unexpected. Jim reacted negatively at first. He thought, "How could Brandon ask for a higher salary when the company is doing terribly?" Jim did not feel that he had the funds to bump Brandon's salary up, but did not want to lose Brandon as an employee. Brandon did not want to leave his job with Jim, but thought that he would be doing a disservice to his family if he did not take the new job and salary. If Jim had his way, Brandon would wait until business got better to get a raise. If Brandon got his way, Jim would match the 15 percent increase.

Brandon and Jim were able to sit down and talk honestly about what each of them wanted. They then problem-solved ways that each of them could get what they thought they needed. Through several honest talks, they were able to work out a bonus situation for Brandon that had the true potential to increase his earnings up to 25 percent. Jim worked to move some of Brandon's low impact assignments to others in the company, thus freeing Brandon up to focus on behaviors at which he excelled. Jim was pleased because he did not have to give a raise to Brandon when money was tight, but was glad to reward Brandon generously if he could increase the profits for the company. Brandon was pleased because they had come up with a solution that would enable him to stay with a company he loved and yet had a realistic opportunity for increasing his earnings. Each of them was very pleased by the arrangement. In the end, Jim's company increased its profitability, and Brandon was given a bonus that was even higher than the 25 percent they had discussed. They both got what they wanted and neither needed to compromise.

Example #7: I hate shopping, but I love you, baby.

Stan hated shopping with a passion. He was a high-powered executive who moved at a lightning-quick pace during the day and could not stand anything that he considered "mundane." Stan's wife, Julie, loved nothing more than clothes shopping. To her, shopping was not just an activity—it was an adventure. For years she had tried to get Stan to share in this activity with her. Sometimes he would tell her to just go without him. Other times he would go and make sure she could see how bored he was by slumping down in the waiting chair and just giving her the "Yeah, yeah, it looks great—get it" response.

One day Julie told him that she didn't want him to go with her anymore, that it wasn't even worth it. Stan was incredulous. "But I go, don't I?" was his response. Julie let him know that while she appreciated him going, she was tired of feeling guilty for asking him to be with her. Something clicked in Stan, and he realized that his behavior was not only wrong, but very selfish. Today, he does not go shopping with Julie unless he can go with the right spirit. When he goes, he goes with a fun and enthusiastic attitude. It isn't because he loves clothes shopping. It is because he loves Julie. And when he goes, he goes because the joy on her face gives him as much pleasure as one of his high-powered business deals.

How it applies

Each of the stories above represents a specific way of dealing with conflict. In my work with disagreements and arguments, I have focused on seven main ways of dealing with a conflictual situation. When dealing with conflict, you can:

- Avoid it
- Give in
- Be passive-aggressive
- Bully the other person
- Compromise
- Problem-solve together with the other person
- Honor the other person

Avoid it

When we avoid conflict completely, we don't even give a chance for resolution. Avoidance can be physical or it can be emotional, like when you ask someone what is wrong and they say, "Nothing," (despite all your senses telling you otherwise). You can avoid it by not answering the phone, not returning an email, ducking down the hall when you see someone coming that you don't want to talk to, not going to a wedding because "you know who" might attend. Or you can avoid just by being emotionally dishonest when someone asks you what you think or how you are feeling. In example #1 above, Cynthia was avoiding conflict by using the caller I.D. to alert her not to pick up her phone.

Give in

Giving in could be viewed as a form of avoidance, but with giving in, at least your wants are out on the table. When we give in, we basically allow someone else to win an argument. We let them have their way despite often feeling bitter about it inside. Sometimes the other person knows that we have given in and sometimes they don't have the slightest clue. In example #2 above, Tom gave in to the person at the service desk despite his frustration and belief that they should make an exception for him.

Be passive-aggressive

Passive-aggressive behavior is just that; it is aggressive behavior that is passive or indirect. The person hints or sends dual messages about his anger rather than being honest about his feelings and asking directly for change. I once worked with a young man who told me that he could always tell growing up when his stepmother was upset. He said that she would never say anything when he upset her. However, without fail, the next morning she would be up at 6:00 in the morning making him breakfast. He found this curious because she never made him breakfast when she was not upset with him, so why would she do it when they were in conflict? The secret is in the fact that he did not get up until 7:30 in the morning, but on these special days she would be up bright and early banging dishes in the kitchen (which was right outside of his room). This invariably woke him up early because of the racket she would generate. On the surface it looked like she was doing something nice for him. Underneath was an anger that she could not be honest about. In the previous example of Steve at the movies, Steve was not quite this passive, but was not as direct as he could have been in asking the moviegoers to be quiet.

Bully the other person

Most of us know what it is like to be bullied. A bully can only see things from one perspective—his. To a bully, the end justifies just about any means. The bully can be very effective at getting what he wants, especially from conflict cowards. In the example above, Patrick was effective in getting his subordinates to at least fake cooperation together, and he didn't care if his style of achieving that goal was disrespectful or not. He had a need and he took care of it, case closed. Unfortunately, there are many bullies both in the business world and at home. They leave destruction in their wake and either don't realize it or don't care. Bullies leave a trail of pain, hurt, and humiliation. It can be effective, but the behavior only serves one person.

Compromise

Compromises are a healthier way to resolve a conflict. In a compromise, you look at each person's stance or position, and each person gives in some to reach a balance between his or her different wishes. Compromises can work well and feel fair to people involved. Unfortunately, in a compromise each person has to give something up. There is a loss for each person involved. The goal of the compromise is to reduce the loss as much as possible and come to a joint decision. In example #5, my wife and I had a compromise that worked well enough for both of us to enjoy our trip to Disney World (we might even go again!). We both gave up some of what we wanted, but we were both also able to achieve something that we wanted. Compromises usually create at least some level of happiness for all people involved.

Problem-solve together

While compromising can be a good thing with positive outcomes, there is a way to deal with conflict that is even more helpful. That approach is problem-solving together. When problem-solving, the goal is that none of the parties involved need to give up what they want. They may give up on a particular way to get something they want, but the discussion around the conflict is a creative exercise. Each person strives to discover the core issue of what each person wants and to find a way that all parties can achieve their desires. The situation cited above with Brandon and Jim in example #6 could have ended very poorly. Fortunately, each of them cared very much about the other person's needs as well as their own. Through taking the time to be kind and creative, they created a true win-win situation.

Honor the other person

To read the above examples you may think that all conflictual situations have to end with everyone getting what they want. That is not true. Sometimes you can actually change what you want. Sometimes you may choose to honor the other person's wishes because honoring them is what you want to do. Honoring can look exactly like giving in, but it is completely opposite in its impact on both the person being honored and the person doing the honoring. When I honor someone, I do the behavior because it pleases me to please the other person. But I do it without bitterness or regret. Rather, I am actually happy to let go of what I previously wanted because it gives me such joy to give the other person what she wants. When I honor, it is also a win-win situation because the other person gets what she wants and I get the complete pleasure of knowing that I was the one to give it. When I honor, I don't keep track of it. I don't save it for later as a leverage point to get the other person to honor me. I do it because the behavior is consistent with the person I want to be. In example #7 above, Stan was a better man for honoring his wife, and she experienced great joy in receiving his care. Their relationship grew tremendously because of it.

Choices are a wonderful part of life, and in conflict you have at least these seven options when you are dealing with different needs or perspectives. Which do you choose? Do you tend to avoid, give in, be passive-aggressive, bully the other person, compromise, problem-solve together, or honor the other person? Through the skills taught in this book, you will increase your ability to make the choice that you truly want to make. You will no longer be on automatic pilot when it comes to conflict. You will have the ability to choose any of the seven ways to respond to conflict. The choice is yours.

Exercises
Self-reflection exercise: What is your habit?
Answer the following questions.

1. Which of the seven ways to handle conflict do you use most frequently?

2. Which of the seven ways to handle conflict do you use most infrequently?

3. Which technique would you like to improve most?

4. What has held you back from using this technique?

5. What is the cost of not changing your automatic behavior?

6. What is the benefit of changing your automatic behavior?

Self-reflection exercise: Cost-benefit analysis
Examine the costs and benefits associated with each approach to conflict.

Approach to conflict	Cost of using this technique	Benefit of using this approach
Avoid		
Give in		
Be passive-aggressive		
Bully the other person		
Compromise		
Problem-solve together		
Honor the other person		

1. As you look at the costs and benefits, what changes do you want to make to how you handle conflict?

2. What makes the difference between giving in and honoring the other person?

Next steps and additional resources

Track your behavior over the next week. Write down each potential conflict situation and record which of the seven choices you made in dealing with the conflict. Start building awareness of how you tend to deal with conflictual situations. Note which occasions you would like to have handled differently.

Analyze the pattern of your behavior to build insight into what you want to change.

For another viewpoint on ways to deal with conflict, try *The Eight Essential Steps to Conflict Resolution* by Dudley Weeks, Ph.D.

"Silence gives consent, or the horrible feeling that nobody's listening."
—Franklin P. Jones

"Man is man because he is free to operate within the framework of his destiny. He is free to deliberate, to make decisions, and to choose between alternatives."
—Martin Luther King Jr.

Chapter 3:

The Top Ten Reasons People Avoid Conflict

There are many reasons that people choose to avoid conflict. In this chapter we will look at ten of the most common fears that people have concerning conflict. We will look at how these fears hold people back even though many times they are based on poor judgements and irrational thinking.

Real life

When I was in high school, I used to spend my summers being a lifeguard at a Christian camp. The campers would come and stay from Sunday to Saturday, and then a new group would come the following Sunday. Many Saturday nights I drove home to stay with my father because the idea of staying in a completely empty camp did not appeal to me. One Saturday I decided to stay overnight. The campground was not well lit in the evenings, and soon after dark I decided to read for a while in my bunk. Eventually my eyes grew tired and I went through the cabin and latched the four doors with the flimsy hooks that were mostly coming out of the wood anyhow.

I was only asleep for about an hour when a loud noise woke me up. It sounded like someone had slammed one of the cabin doors. I laid in my bed somewhat startled and cursing myself for having turned out all of the lights. Imagine a long cabin with about fifty bunk beds lined up on each side, where visibility was highly limited. My bunk was all the way at the end by the bathroom, so if someone were down at the other end, there was no way I could see him. After long minutes of playing out several "psycho killer comes to isolated camp in the woods to kill lifeguard" scenarios, I finally summoned the courage to feel my way to the light switch.

Once I turned on the lights, I checked under the beds to find nothing except the usual dust bunnies that populated the cement floors. As I made my way to the doors, I found that one of them was open. The latch was on the floor and, given that no one was in the cabin, I figured that a strong gust of wind must have blown the door open. Even though my handyman skills are about on par with my ability to play professional football, I was able to fix the door enough to latch it again. With my explanation for the loud noise firmly accepted in my brain, I was able to get back to bed. Again, within an hour I was woken by another loud noise. My first hypothesis was that the wind had blown the door open again because I could hear that the weather outside was somewhat violent. That's when I heard the sound that stopped my heart.

Can you imagine what sandy boots might sound like on a cement floor? Think for a second and bring that sound to mind. I heard that scraping sound as I lay frozen in my bed. And while I felt safer by pulling the covers over my head, it probably was a flimsy defense strategy against the lifeguard killer. Eventually, I managed to get out of the bed and grab a broom, but the sound stopped and a new sound began—the sound of the Beach Boys. Now, hearing the Beach Boys may not sound frightening to you, but then you probably don't know that I had a Beach Boys cassette in my car that was parked outside the cabin. Could the lifeguard killer have broken into my locked car to play the Beach Boys? What kind of sick individual was I dealing with? As these thoughts entered my mind, I got back into my bed and lay there in fear for much of the night. I just couldn't go out and face whatever was out in my car. My exhausted mind eventually fell back asleep for the night after lots of prayer and the eventual ceasing of "Surfin' USA."

The next morning I awoke to find the cabin door once again open. As I searched around the cabin, I heard the scraping sound again. I finally figured out that it was coming from the bathroom. However, when I investigated I found out that it was merely the curtain brushing against the window screen in the wind. With this new information, I went outside to find my car still locked with no sign of entry. After several decades of trying to figure out what happened that night, my best hypothesis is that the wind created all of the thoughts in my mind and perhaps some country folk from nearby farms enjoyed loudly played Beach Boys music. The whole "camp psycho killer" scenario was played out in my young head with little grounding in reality.

How it applies

It is amazing what our minds can do. We can create terror for ourselves with our imagination. While sometimes what we imagine does come true, many times it does not. In the story above I was able to paralyze myself with my overactive imagination—enough so that I avoided fully checking out the sounds I was hearing which would have revealed the truth to me and given me a much more relaxing evening. Often, the reasons that we avoid conflict are not completely based on reality. They are often based on irrational fears. I have found that the following top ten fears often contribute to conflict:

1) Fear of harm
2) Fear of rejection
3) Fear of loss of relationship
4) Fear of anger
5) Fear of being seen as selfish
6) Fear of saying the wrong thing
7) Fear of failing
8) Fear of hurting someone else
9) Fear of getting what you want
10) Fear of intimacy

Fear of harm

Human beings have a built in fight-or-flight instinct, and many times the wiser person will take the flight option. It is smart to avoid a dangerous area of a city that you have never been to before. It shows wisdom to get out of a physically abusive relationship. It is admirable to stay out of emotionally abusive relationships. However, sometimes we have a flight response in reaction to a false perception of harm. In our minds we can exaggerate the emotional harm someone can cause us in a relationship. The more we exaggerate the harm, the more likely it is that we will avoid the conflict. This explains why some people are better able to face conflict with general acquaintances than with loved ones. The more we love and respect someone, the more vulnerable we feel to being emotionally hurt by his or her reaction. On the other hand, facing conflict is most important to do with those with whom we want intimate relationships. Therefore, we often need to risk getting hurt feelings in order to bring the relationship to a deeper level.

Fear of rejection

Some conflict cowards avoid conflict because there is a fear of being rejected by the other person. They fear that the other person will withdraw his love or push them away. This leads to more than hurt feelings because of the feelings of abandonment it creates. Individuals who have a family history of abandonment or shame often live with a fear of rejection. Again, this fear plays out most intensely with the people who we love the most. Their rejection is much more powerful than the rejection of a stranger. And again we are stuck with the intimacy paradox. If we don't risk rejection, then we cannot gain true acceptance. If you are in a relationship with someone you love and you suppress your needs and feelings, then that person is only accepting a façade of you. Until you face the potential conflict, you always will wonder subconsciously if he would still love the "true" you.

Fear of loss of relationship

The fear of rejection can be taken up a notch by looking at the fear of totally losing the relationship. The end result of the total rejection of a person is the loss of the relationship. Some conflict cowards hide their true desires because maintaining the relationship is more important than getting what they want. These individuals are trapped into believing that their worth is dependent on the other person accepting them and staying with them. In the healthiest of relationships you are not with others because you need them, but rather you are with them because you want them. When I can feel worthwhile as an individual, then I can be completely honest in a close relationship. Betraying myself is not worth the reward of maintaining a relationship in which I cannot fully be who I am and who I want to be.

Fear of anger

A fourth fear that is related to avoiding conflict is fear of anger. Many conflict cowards do not like hearing someone who is angry. They may know that the person will not hurt them, reject them, or leave them, but they just can't stand to witness anger. Often, these individuals grew up in homes that showed unhealthy attitudes regarding anger. Either anger was never allowed (so it is seen as terrible), or anger spewed forth out of control and had negative consequences on the family members. In truth, anger is just anger. It is just a feeling that we feel when we perceive an injustice occurring. People who are confident and secure in their relationships can allow the other person to get angry without fear. Conflict cowards can actually cause more anger in someone by avoiding the possibility of making him angry. I have worked with many clients who become extremely frustrated when they know that something is wrong with the other person, but they cannot get the other person to admit it. It is a wonderful gift to allow someone to be angry at you and to make that OK, rather than implying that their anger is wrong. I am, of course, referring to the emotion of anger and not to actions of anger that can be destructive.

Fear of being seen as selfish

The previous four fears were based on the reactions of other people. Sometimes we are not afraid of their actions, but rather we fear their interpretation of the situation. We fear that they will see us as selfish. What messages were you given as a child about selfishness? If this is one of your fears, then you may have received shame messages in your youth whenever you were perceived as being selfish. But what is selfishness? Is it wrong to have a need, feeling, or want and to express it? I don't think so. In chapter 20 we will discuss this issue in more detail, but for now I just want to make a distinction between *asking* for what you want versus feeling *entitled* to always get what you want. There is absolutely nothing wrong with asking for what you want. In fact, if you never ask for what you want, then you are depriving people around you from being able to give to you most effectively. However, the person who feels that his wants should all be fulfilled, despite what anyone else wants, falls into the selfishness category. If you were shamed growing up for expressing wants, you might want to examine how fear of appearing selfish contributes to your conflict avoidance.

Fear of saying the wrong thing

Sometimes we are not as afraid of the other person's actions as we are of our own. The next five fears deal with fears about how we react to the conflict rather than the other person. Often, conflict avoiders fear that if they finally take the "cork out of the bottle" then all of the anger will come flying out and they will say something regrettable. Rather than risk "foot in mouth" disease, they contain their frustration. Ironically, the containment of anger and frustration often leads to the very thing the person feared. They get fed up, and the anger spews out all over the other person. Their technique for avoiding the feared response actually creates the feared response. Fortunately, you can learn to diminish this fear by practicing your confrontation using skills discussed later. As they say, practice makes perfect.

Fear of failing

What if you confront the other person and it does not work? Before the confrontation, at least allow yourself the luxury of imagining a positive response if you were to speak up. That illusion could disappear if you actually confront the person. This illusion is, for some, a secret haven, a hidden comfort that allows the relationship to maintain a status quo of safety. Others just assume that the confrontation will fail, and thus it is not worth the emotional energy it takes to deal with the other person. Fear of failing can impact us in many areas of our life. The most successful people have a unique perspective on failure. These successful people reframe failure as a learning experience. Thus from every failed attempt you can learn something that will increase the odds for success in the future. Learning is much less frightening than failing. If you do practice the skills in this book and you don't get immediate results, I encourage you to learn from the event. In fact, learn from each confrontation you have. If you learn from it, then it is not a failure.

Fear of hurting someone else

Related to the conflict coward's fear of saying the wrong thing is the fear of hurting someone else. Many conflict cowards are extremely sensitive and caring individuals who would never purposely hurt a fly. In fact, many would much rather experience hurt themselves than to risk harm to another person. While this may sound admirable, it really is not. I used to be one of these individuals myself. Friends would try to help me change by telling me not to care so much about the other person. That strategy was doomed to fail with me because much of my identity is wrapped up in caring for others, and I like that about myself. However, one supervisor I had in my therapy training had a different perspective on my behavior. He told me that it was disrespectful of me to think that I had to protect the other person. He firmly chastised me that I obviously thought very little about the other person if I believed that I was so powerful that they would crumble at my words. While I didn't like his interpretation (in fact, ironically, I was a little hurt by it) he was right. Now I strive to respect other people enough to confront them in a healthy way and trust that they will be able to deal with it. I grew from this supervisor's willingness to hurt my feelings. Who am I to cheat others from that?

Fear of getting what you want

On the opposite end of the fear of failure is the fear of success. Some individuals are actually afraid of getting what they want, so they subconsciously make sure that they never get it! Why in the world would they do this? Well, there may be several reasons. People may not feel that they deserve to get what they want. Again this often can relate to messages that we have carried within ourselves since childhood, especially a childhood with some form of deprivation. To get what we want feels strange and awkward. To live in a constant state of wanting something that we don't have just feels more known or comfortable. For others, they may be afraid of the consequences of getting what they want. Maybe they fear that they will owe someone or perhaps even that others would expect more from them if they had what they wanted. To avoid that responsibility, they avoid asking for what they need or desire.

Fear of intimacy

The final and probably most subconscious of the fears that impact us in conflict is the fear of intimacy. Hopefully I have been able to make a case for the fact that conflict is necessary to create a truly intimate relationship. Therefore it stands to reason that one of the best ways to avoid genuine intimacy is to avoid disagreement, differing needs, and general conflict. People who fear intimacy keep their dreams, desires, and wants close to the vest. They may know what they want, but no one else may have a clue. This tendency can be particularly frustrating for the other person in a relationship with the conflict coward. The lack of conflict hurts the relationship and guarantees that intimacy will only go to a certain level and never as far as it could go.

Do you recognize yourself in any of the ten fears that cause people to avoid conflict? As stated earlier, our fear is often just in our heads. This doesn't make it any less real, but it does mean that we can change it. However, for most, identifying the problem is not enough to fully change it. Insight is often a necessary first step, but it is not the final answer. In chapter 5 we will look at a strategy for tackling our perceptions and looking at conflict in a new way. Before we do that, however, we have to ask an important question in the next chapter: Why change?

Exercises
Self-reflection exercise: Rate your fear

On a scale of 1 to 10, rate how much you experience each of the ten fears when considering facing a conflict.

(1 = Not at all; 5 = Somewhat; 10 = Extremely fearful):

Fear of harm	_____
Fear of rejection	_____
Fear of loss of relationship	_____
Fear of anger	_____
Fear of being seen as selfish	_____
Fear of saying the wrong thing	_____
Fear of failing	_____
Fear of hurting someone else	_____

Fear of getting what you want   _____

Fear of intimacy   _____

Self-challenge exercise: Check your honesty with yourself

What is your top fear in terms of facing conflict?

How much is this fear based on realistic evidence?

How much of this fear could be just your perception?

How could you find out if your fears are real in a safe manner?

What can you do to deal with this fear?

Next steps and additional resources

Within a safe context, find one situation this week where you are feeling fear of conflict. Analyze which of the ten fears is holding you back. Take one step toward facing your fear. Try to make just a little progress. Be a scientist and study the results of this experiment.

To understand how shame from the past impacts current living, try *Healing The Shame That Binds You* by John Bradshaw.

> *"I believe that anyone can conquer fear by doing the things*
> *he fears to do, provided he keeps doing them until he gets*
> *a record of successful experiences behind him."*
> —Eleanor Roosevelt

Chapter 4

Why Change?

In previous chapters we explored possible reasons that you may choose to avoid conflict. The fact is that you will not change the way you deal with conflict until you have a good reason to change. This reason has to make sense to you and not because someone else tells you to do it. In this chapter we will focus on potential reasons for changing how you deal with conflict.

Real life

"Why don't you fight back?" his aunt asked. "You should not let the other kids treat you that way." The little boy did not know how to answer her. He didn't know why he didn't fight back, he just knew that it was easier to curl up in his seat and take the ribbing than to risk a bigger confrontation with the boys. He was a pretty good kid and just wanted everyone to get along. He couldn't fathom why the other kids were mean to him, and fighting back had never crossed his mind. That was his preschool year. He was already a conflict coward.

"Do you know the boys who did this to you?" asked his father. The boy, now a whopping twelve years old, did know the three boys that threatened him. "Yes," he answered with much apprehension. "Can you take one of them in a fight?" his father asked, leaving the boy with two mental choices. Tell the truth and watch his father's disappointment wash over his face like a tidal wave, or lie through his teeth and hope that his dad was merely asking a hypothetical question in order to explore the infinite possibilities that existed for fixing the situation. The boy decided to place his bet on the hypothetical exploration reason and thus stammered out a "yes" to his obviously scientifically curious father. "OK, jump in the car and let's find him."

"Find who?" was the immediate reaction from the boy, who then realized that his dad was on the warpath and not in the mood to explore hypotheses concerning young men and confidence in violent situations. While his father (a pastor by profession, but obviously more of an "eye for an eye" kind of person than a "turn the other cheek" type guy) was driving furiously around town on a seek-and-have-my-son-destroy mission, the boy was praying. He was secretly praying to God that all three boys were enjoying home-cooked meals in the comfort of their homes and that they would be nowhere to be found.

After twenty minutes of searching, the pair returned home. "Sorry, I couldn't find them, son," stated the gladiator-like father. The son merely shrugged his shoulders and went off to his room. There he promised God his entire allowance for the next month for successfully hiding these boys who would have surely beaten him to a bloody and humiliated pulp. The boy was still a conflict coward.

The same boy, now a young man, was sitting in his graduate level class with a teacher who was feared by many of the students. Frustrated with the class, the professor chastised the students by calling them lazy and stupid. The young man had spent several nights with little-to-no sleep and was not in the mood to be falsely criticized. In his most passive-aggressive style, he closed his notebook, put down his pen, and intently glared at the instructor. To his astonishment, the professor did not crumble and fall apart from this approach. Several students gathered after the class complaining to each other about the comment. The young man suggested that they go to the professor and tell him that they were not happy. He was dismissed and told that it would not do any good and that this professor was the type that would hold it against you. "Don't do it" was the strong advice. However, for some strange reason the young man could not let the comment drop.

After class, the young man forced himself to go to the professor's office. Sitting across from this man who had great power over his career, the young man barely managed to get out the words, "I am not lazy or stupid, and I, uh, didn't appreciate you saying that in class." He quickly looked away from the professor as if expecting a blow (a verbal blow, but a blow nonetheless). Several seconds ticked by, and the young man slowly looked up. As their eyes locked, the professor, in total humility, said, "I'm sorry. I was frustrated, but that was wrong of me to say." The young man was completely stunned. From that day on, there was a mutual respect between the two that lasted throughout his graduate training experience. It was a lesson in facing conflict that he never forgot.

That young man was a conflict coward for most of his life. I know him well because that young man was me.

How it applies

"Why do *I* have to change?" This is a question my clients often ask me when attempting to learn how to deal better with conflict. My answer is always the same. "You don't *have to* change, it is completely your choice." I answer that way because it's the truth. You can live out the rest of your life as a conflict coward and probably do OK for yourself. However, with all choices come consequences, and the best way to deal with "Why change?" is to really look at "Why do I want to change?" There is some reason that you picked up this book. What was it? Some possibilities:

- You are tired of keeping your thoughts and feelings inside.
- You see how conflict avoidance has hurt you.
- You are hurting a relationship by avoiding conflict.
- You are the recipient of bullying and you are tired of it.
- Someone bought this book as a gift for you so you would get the hint.

Whatever the reason, it is important that you fully explore why you are holding this book in your hands. For many of you, your more primal instincts will be saying, "Put it down. You don't have to change. Change is dangerous!" These are the instincts that have caused you to avoid dealing with conflict.

For me, the change from being a conflict-avoider to someone who faces conflict came gradually. I grew up with stomach problems (I was diagnosed at twelve with an ulcer), which I believe were due to my internalizing my emotions. What I didn't realize until I was older is that the internalizing of my emotions and subsequent lack of confidence was a magnet for predators.

Unknowingly, I attracted conflict to myself by wearing a big emotional bulls-eye on my back. "Come kick me, I won't fight back" was an invitation for bullies everywhere. My greatest desire was to avoid conflict, though I was actually a walking invitation for it.

As I entered college, I started to become aware of how avoiding conflict had hurt me growing up. As I entered graduate school, I felt like passivity would be my downfall. So I started being more assertive—not perfectly and certainly not always, but more than I ever had been in my entire life. Amazingly, I found that a more active approach to my life made my life better. Also, nine times out of ten, the response that I was afraid of getting from the other person never happened. In fact, people often apologized or backed off when I confronted them. I just couldn't believe it. So I spent years practicing how to say things to people in a way that they could hear them. I have become convinced that so much of my success is due to my willingness to say the truth to others in a loving way.

That briefly describes my journey with conflict. What is your journey? How has being a conflict coward hurt you? How could your life change if you handled conflict with grace and confidence? Have you painted a bulls-eye on your back for bullies? Only you know the answers and only you can decide. I realize that it is a tough decision. If you have acted one way for decades, it is very hard to learn a new way. However, it is not impossible! This book is built from the beginning to the end for the person who is afraid of conflict. I will walk you through a step-by-step process for change. Right now, all you have to do is decide if you want to change. You don't have to know how. You don't even have to decide the pace yet. You just need to decide what you want to do. The following exercises are here to help you make the best decision for yourself.

Exercises
Self-reflection exercise: Why change?
Take the time to actually write out your reasons for changing the way that you deal with conflict. Complete the three statements below and refer back to them as you work through this book.

I want to change the way I deal with conflict because...

If I change the way that I deal with conflict, my life will improve in that I...

When facing conflict starts getting uncomfortable, I will remind myself that...

Self-reflection exercise: Personal goals

Write out some general goals that you have in mind when it comes to dealing with conflict. These goals may change as you learn more from your reading, but will serve as a good starting point to help you focus on how you can apply what you are reading. Here are some examples:

- When I have an argument with my spouse, I want to always say how I feel in a way that is respectful, yet strong.
- When I am unhappy with my meal at a restaurant, I want to ask the server to bring me something else.
- When a coworker is rude to me, I want to bring it to his attention and ask him to be more respectful.
- When my boss does not notice my contribution, I want to bring it to her attention.
- I will tell my sister to stop bringing up that story from the past that embarrasses me every time the family gets together.
- I will tell my colleague how his lateness to meetings impacts me in a way that is caring, but direct.
- I will quit agreeing to go out with people who I don't really enjoy being with.

Those are some general examples. Now what are three goals of your own?

1.

2.

3.

Next steps and additional resources

In order to give yourself some accountability, call a friend and share your goals and reasons for changing how you deal with conflict. Ask him or her to check in with you from time to time to help keep you on track. Ask if you can call for support when this journey becomes uncomfortable for you. Also, take a few minutes each day to imagine how your life could shift for the positive if you learn to face your fear of conflict. Imagine your confidence increasing as you practice and grow in your skills.

For a general source to help you take control of your life, try *Unlock Your Personal Potential: A Self-Coaching Workbook* by Richard Bisiker.

"Bravery is being the only one who knows that you are afraid."
—Franklin P. Jones

"To have courage for whatever comes in life—everything lies in that."
—Mother Teresa

How to Motivate Yourself to Deal with Conflict

Chapter 5:

The Secret for Making Yourself Face Conflict

Henry Ford said, "Whether you think you can or you think you can't, you're right." Our beliefs and perceptions decide much of our success in life. In this chapter we will explore this concept and walk through a technique for creating realistic and helpful self-beliefs.

Real life

Claire hated conflict. She had grown up in a home where harsh words flew fast and furious. Her father tended to be an outwardly passive man who showed his aggression toward Claire's mother in thinly disguised criticisms. These subtle insults concerning Claire's mother's weight and physical attractiveness were said with outward humor, but never failed to create the same predictable reaction from her mother. Claire's mother had an opposite style of conflict from her father. She, in contrast, was a very vocal woman who expressed her displeasure impulsively, aggressively, and frequently.

Claire's father knew just the right buttons to push, and Claire's mother impulsively reacted to his comments in a loud and dramatic style. Claire watched the two of them bicker at each other constantly and would often end up as a target for both of them if she tried to interfere. As she grew up, Claire vowed that her life would be more peaceful and that she would not have such conflict in her life. It had been too painful.

Claire married soon after college and started a successful career as a mid-level manager in a large corporation. As the years rolled by, Claire did everything she could to avoid conflict at home and at work. In both places Claire quickly would suppress her own desires for the desires of her husband, boss, or coworkers. If anyone started to escalate a discussion toward a potential conflict, Claire would either quickly give in or remove herself from the situation. This avoidant tendency worked in the short-term by removing immediate conflicts, but had negative effects on Claire's relationships. Her husband became increasingly frustrated that his wife would never tell him what she wanted. She always would make him decide where they went to eat, how they spent their holidays, and where they went on vacation. Then she would subtly show disappointment until her husband confronted her and she would put on a false act of support for their activity. At work, coworkers started taking advantage of her compliance by asking special favors and never giving them in return. Her boss started to rely on her more with tight deadlines and started taking her extra effort for granted.

Eventually, Claire became more and more upset as she felt that others never cared about what she wanted. Her inner tension started showing up in the form of shorter frustration tolerance. On one occasion she even left an important meeting in tears because no one seemed to appreciate the effort that she had put in on a project. To the shock of everyone, she eventually quit her job and went to a different company into a position of less responsibility. Her marriage also suffered as her husband became more and more vocal about the lack of intimacy he felt with his wife. Claire's plan had backfired. Instead of creating less conflict in her life, her avoidant tendencies had created more.

How it applies

You can't really blame Claire for trying. Not many people really enjoy conflict. Claire, like many of us, likes to avoid pain and for her (and maybe you, too), conflict is pain! This is especially true if your models for communication (usually parents) showed a destructive style for trying to work out differences. If conflict means pain, then you will avoid it at all costs. This is why many of us accidentally cause such emotional pain for ourselves by becoming conflict-avoiders. The pain could take the form of failed relationships or it could even take the form of physical illness from all of our contained emotions. Our very attempts at decreasing pain in our lives can cause us pain. It is in this paradox that the secret to facing conflict resides.

As I have stated in previous chapters, it wasn't until I went to college that I learned to handle myself in conflictual situations. There was a secret that I discovered there that completely changed the way I dealt with differences and disagreements. This secret exposes the paradox that binds you to avoiding conflict. The secret to changing the way that you deal with conflict is this. Get ready, it is really profound.

> Avoiding the conflict had to be more painful than facing it, and facing the conflict had to be more pleasurable than avoiding it.

Sound too easy? OK, well, there is a secret beneath the secret. Have you ever had a dream where you were falling off a cliff, or out of the bed, or any other variation of that theme? Those of you who have had this dream know what happens. Your body jolts in the bed as if you were actually falling. Isn't this kind of crazy? You aren't falling, yet your body freaks out in the bed. (I've scared my wife a few times with this type of dream). Your mind cannot tell the difference between the illusion that you are falling and the reality that you are nice and comfy in your bed. In other words, our perceptions are more important than our reality.

We can create all sorts of bodily reactions just by thinking of certain things. Imagine sucking on a juicy, yellow lemon and you can make yourself drool on your shirt. Think about the last really funny scene that you saw in a movie and you can feel a pleasant feeling well up inside of you. Think about all the horrible things that will go wrong if you speak the truth to someone who might get angry and feel your fear build. Our minds have such incredible power. Therefore the "true" pain and pleasure of facing conflict doesn't really matter. What matters is your perception of the pain and pleasure that you will experience if you confront the conflict. So, the full secret is this: When your *perception* of the pain of avoiding conflict and the pleasure of facing it are greater than your *perception* of the pain of facing conflict and the pleasure of avoiding it, you will face it.

To understand this better, let's use the example of exercise (don't groan, this one gets me, too). When you think about developing an exercise program, you need to weigh the pain and pleasure that it will cause you. What are the

issues around doing exercise and what are the concepts that will help motivate you to do it? Consider the chart below.

Pain of exercising	Pleasure of avoiding exercising
Issue: It's painful	Issue: Get to sleep in
Issue: Have to get up early	Issue: Get to do other things I enjoy more
Issue: Takes up my time	Issue: It is easier
Issue: Hate to sweat	Issue: Can relax
Pain of avoiding exercising	**Pleasure of exercising**
Concept: I could die earlier	Concept: Less guilt
Concept: Clothes don't fit	Concept: Feel better
Concept: Don't feel good about myself	Concept: Look better
Concept: Have less energy	Concept: Will be comfortable in my clothes
Concept: Breathe hard tying my shoes	Concept: Positive attention from others

In this chart we see several different factors involved in the consideration
of building an exercise program. The top row represents several issues that
could keep you from exercising, while the bottom row gives many concepts
that would motivate someone to exercise or start and keep their fitness program. The person who does not exercise is keeping his focus on the issues in
the top row. In his mind, he only sees:

Pain of exercising	Pleasure of avoiding exercising
Issue: It's painful	Issue: Get to sleep in
Issue: Have to get up early	Issue: Get to do other things I enjoy more
Issue: Takes up my time	Issue: It is easier
Issue: Hate to sweat	Issue: Can relax

He does not focus on the bottom row, and therefore fails to do a consistent exercise program. The perception of the pain of exercising and the pleasure of avoiding it outweighs the pain of avoiding exercise and the pleasure of doing it. The person who exercises on a regular basis will keep his focus on the bottom row.

Pain of avoiding exercising	Pleasure of exercising
Concept: I could die earlier	Concept: Less guilt
Concept: Clothes don't fit	Concept: Feel better
Concept: Don't feel good about myself	Concept: Look better
Concept: Have less energy	Concept: Will be comfortable in my clothes
Concept: Breathe hard tying my shoes	Concept: Positive attention from others

This focus enables the person to stay motivated and on track with his goals and aspirations. It is not necessarily true that the issues in the top row are any less real than the concepts in the bottom row. It is merely the person's conscious decision to focus on the concepts that will help him lead a healthier and happier life in the long run. The perception of pain and pleasure works to aid the person to care for himself rather than hold him back and eventually hurt his health and energy.

Exercise is not the only area of life that is governed by our perceptions of pain and pleasure. We can easily apply the same concepts to conflictual situations. As long as your perception of the pain of facing conflict and the pleasure of avoiding it is greater than your perception of the pain of avoiding conflict and the pleasure of facing it, you are doomed to be a conflict-avoider. However, the wonderful thing about all of this is that you can take control of your perceptions!

Let's apply the same concept of pain and pleasure to your personal issues and concepts related to conflict situations. Fill in the following boxes to understand your perceptions. I've started you off with a few to jolt your thinking. Feel free to cross them out if they do not apply to you:

The pain and pleasure of conflict

Pain of facing conflict	Pleasure of avoiding conflict
Issue: They might yell at me.	Issue: I'll feel relieved.
Issue: I might say something that I'll regret.	Issue: It is safer.
Issue:	Issue:
Issue:	Issue:
Issue:	Issue:
Issue:	Issue:
Issue:	Issue:
Pain of avoiding conflict	**Pleasure of facing conflict**
Concept: The problem will just continue.	Concept: It at least creates the possibility of a better situation.
Concept: I feel like a coward.	Concept: I will feel proud of myself.
Concept:	Concept:
Concept:	Concept:
Concept:	Concept:
Concept:	Concept:
Concept:	Concept:

Looking at the above chart (go back and fill it out if you haven't already), you can see why you avoid conflict. These automatic thoughts can control your behavior. Therefore, we don't stop with just looking at your automatic perceptions. Rather, this is where you start empowering yourself to impact your perceptions to improve your life. You can create this through a process of problem-solving solutions and expanding your focus. By creating possible solutions for the first row of the pain/pleasure chart, you decrease the power of the things that hold you back. Usually when you avoid conflict you are allowing these perceptions to go unchallenged and thus they control your behavior. Your solutions help decrease the power of these self-defeating thoughts. Taking the avoidance-producing thoughts from above, we could do the following chart.

Pain/Pleasure chart

Pain of facing conflict

Issue: They might yell at me.

Solution: Develop a plan for handling it if it occurs, such as letting them know you will come back and talk to them when they will be more respectful.

Issue: I might say something that I'll regret.

Solution: Write what you want to say in advance. The second you start straying from your plan, interrupt the conversation, admit that you are not handling it the way you want to, and then say it differently.

Pleasure of avoiding conflict

Issue: I'll feel relieved.

Solution: Focus on the fact that the relief is only temporary. Get your goal of true relief by dealing effectively with the conflict.

Issue: It is safer.

Solution: Remind yourself that you are only creating the illusion of safety. Internally, you are hurting and are anything but safe.

Next we take the perceptions in the bottom row of our pain/pleasure chart and we build them up or expand them. Using the same examples from our previous chart, we can do the following.

Pain of avoiding conflict

Concept: The problem will just continue.

Expand: Do I really want to live like this forever? I'm keeping my own misery going by allowing this problem to continue without ever trying to change it. The only way I'll have a chance for real peace is to use all of my wisdom and skills to handle this.

Concept: I feel like a coward.

Expand: How do I feel when I keep my mouth shut in these situations? What could that be doing to my self-esteem? I am much more courageous than I think.

Pleasure of facing conflict

Concept: It at least creates the possibility of a better situation.

Expand: What would I feel like if we were able to resolve this conflict and not have to deal with it anymore? How might my life look different? My happiness is worth the chance. Think of other times that you confronted a problem situation and improved your life by doing so.

Concept: I will feel proud of myself.

Expand: Think of the last time you did something that you felt proud of. How can you apply some of the same things/behaviors to the current situation? What lessons did you learn about yourself when you did something in spite of its difficulty?

Some of you may be wondering what happens if the reasons for avoiding conflict are really more powerful than the reasons for facing the situation. If that is the case, then the answer probably lies elsewhere than directly confronting the conflict. For example, if confronting the conflict may cause physical harm, then avoiding it might be a better option. An extreme example of this is when an abused spouse needs to go to a shelter rather than stand up to a physically abusive husband or wife. Another example might be if confronting a work situation directly would likely lead to getting fired or someone making each day a living hell for you. A better option might be to talk with the human resources department. The bottom line is that this process will help lead you to a solid decision on whether or not it truly is in your best interests to confront the problem. You will know the answer that is right for you after fully going through the process of looking at all of the issues and concepts involved using the charts provided.

Exercises
Solo Exercise: Determining all the issues and concepts and moving to action

For this exercise we will take all of the information, insights, and learning from the charts that you filled out earlier. Use the following blank charts to rewrite the issues that cause you to avoid conflict and the concepts that will help you face the situation. Problem-solve each of the fears/issues in the first row and expand on the concepts in the second row. Do this in as much detail as possible in order to motivate yourself to take the next step in your growth in changing your cowardly ways!

Pain of facing conflict

Issue:
Solution:

Issue:
Solution:

Issue:
Solution:

Issue:
Solution:

Issue:
Solution:

Pleasure of avoiding conflict

Issue:
Solution:

Issue:
Solution:

Issue:
Solution:

Issue:
Solution:

Issue:
Solution:

Pain of avoiding conflict

Concept:
Expand:

Concept:
Expand:

Concept:
Expand:

Pleasure of facing conflict

Concept:
Expand:

Concept:
Expand:

Concept:
Expand:

Concept:

Expand:

Concept:

Expand:

Concept:

Expand:

Concept:

Expand:

Concept:

Expand:

Concept:

Expand:

Concept:

Expand:

Concept:

Expand:

Next steps and additional resources

Take your sheet of expanded concepts and put it where you can read it every day (i.e., your daytimer, a mirror, etc.). Constantly remind yourself of the reasons that you will benefit from facing conflict. It is crucial that you do this because just reading this chapter *is not* going to change years of an ingrained habit. To take control of your habit, these concepts must be kept at the forefront of your conscious mind.

For those of you who are really ambitious, you could make an audio tape of these motivating concepts and put them on a looping tape to listen to in the car or at home, or even while you are sleeping. Start the process of reversing those old self-defeating issues today!

For more on the relationship between pain and pleasure and human motivation, try *Awaken the Giant Within* by Anthony Robbins.

"Courage is grace under pressure."

—Ernest Hemingway

Chapter 6:

Confronting Your Fear One Step at a Time

Some people like to get into a cool swimming pool by diving in. They like to take the shock initially and get use to the water more quickly. Others have a more methodical style of getting used to the cool water. They prefer to start with their feet, move deeper up to their knees, stop for awhile, move on up to their stomach, and then to their chest, before finally taking the plunge and sticking their head underwater. There is not a right way and a wrong way to get into a swimming pool, just different ways. People also have different ways of confronting fear. In this chapter we will examine how to face fear one step at a time.

Real life

"It's only an ant!" I said in my best authoritative father voice. "You are bigger than the ant, it will not hurt you!" I emphasized. My five-year-old son, who was the recipient of my admonition, simply looked at me with even greater fear in his eyes. You see, I was rushing to get to a store before it closed, and while attempting to get in the car my son noticed an ant by the door. For some strange reason he was afraid to get in the car because the ant was "blocking the door" (how something the size of a small breadcrumb could "block" the door is baffling to me, but I'm just reporting, not interpreting). My son screamed in terror at the sight of this vicious and obviously "deadly" insect. Shamefully, my immediate response was one of frustration. I was in a hurry, and his behavior was so irrational that I jumped all over him verbally.

As most of you can guess, my loud voice and exasperated comments merely served to build his fear. By the end of my short tirade, he was more frightened of this critter than he was to begin with. Fortunately, I quickly came to my senses and decided to take a better approach.

The first thing that I did was apologize to my son for taking out my frustration on him. Then I started talking softly and pleasantly and told him that I was going to pick up the ant and keep it far away from him. Then, as the ant was crawling on my hand, I asked him if I could get closer. When he started showing curiosity, I got even closer. Each time I moved closer I promised him that I was not going to allow the ant to get on him. The last step was to ask him to touch the ant, which he did briefly. Then I set the ant back down on the ground and we got in the car and went on our merry way.

Within a week he was stomping on ants left and right and declaring his dominion over them! Then we had a lesson about how to treat living creatures, but that is another story.

How it applies

How many times has someone told you to "just get over" your fear of conflict? Besides being a somewhat simplistic psychological intervention, "Just get over it" just doesn't work. Think about it; when is the last time you told someone to "just get over it" and they responded, "Wow, thanks! You're right, my fear is completely irrational! Whew, I feel like a new man. No more fear for me!"

It's completely ludicrous to even consider, isn't it? Yet, often the best pseudo-therapeutic advice we receive is the equivalent of "get over it."

True conflict cowards know that fearing conflict is not simply a matter of choice. In other words, you can't just decide one day not to be afraid. It's like the person who has been in a bad car accident. The next time that he starts to get in a car, he is going to feel fear or anxiety. However, most people go ahead and get in the car, and after a few times the fear diminishes and eventually disappears. On less frequent occasions the person may feel the fear as they start to get in the car and decide not to drive. They decide to avoid the action that is causing them to feel afraid. Do you have any idea what that does to the fear? Avoiding fear actually *increases* the fear. You then feel this increase the next time you start to confront the situation. It also increases your chances for avoiding the action again.

Avoidance = increased fear for the future = increased chances for
avoidance behavior

The psychobabble term for this is "negative reinforcement." Negative reinforcement occurs when your behavior results in something negative being
taken away. Since the negative thing is taken away, you feel temporarily better and therefore your avoidance behavior is reinforced. So not getting in the
car after an accident feels good temporarily and thus increases the odds that
you will avoid getting in the car the next time. In addition, the fear is reinforced so that the next time you start to get in the car, your fear is worse. If
this person were to avoid getting in the car time after time, then the fear
would be built up to a level that would be impossible to "just get over it."

How long have you been a conflict-avoider? A couple years? A couple
decades? If so, the bad news is that you probably can't just get over it. However, the good news is that you can deal with the fear by taking it one step
at a time.

Remember the example with my son who was afraid of the vicious, neck-
fanging, face-eating, little boy–kidnapping ant? I slowly introduced the ant,
getting closer and closer to him as I felt he was ready to deal with it. He had
a little fear each time, but not the overwhelming fear that had the neighbors
wondering if I was stringing him up and torturing him in the garage. The
process that I used was based on something called systematic desensitization
(I know, I'm using psychobabble again, but stick with me). With systematic
desensitization, you build a hierarchy of what you fear and then slowly deal
with each of the fears one at a time, starting with the thing that you fear least.

With my son, the hierarchy was based on distance away from the ant.
When talking about fear of conflict, we have to look at things more
abstractly. So, for example, are you more afraid of confronting your boss or
confronting your significant other? Are you more afraid of returning a
defective item in the store or telling your hairdresser that you don't like the
way she cut your hair last time? Are you more afraid of telling your teenager
that he has to make curfew or he doesn't get the car for the weekend or your
coworker that you are frustrated when she is late to important meetings?
Another way to look at levels of fear is to take one situation with different

levels of confrontation. For example, let's say that you are afraid to tell your coworker that you feel she monopolizes team meeting time on her own department's issues and that she changes the subject when you bring out issues concerning your own department. Starting with the least threatening action, your fear hierarchy could look like this:

- Send a memo in advance listing several issues that you would like to bring up about your department in the meeting.
- Send an email to your coworker in advance of the meeting asking her to support you in the team meeting when you bring up the issues (since you often run out of time in the meetings).
- Talk with your coworker before the meeting and let her know that you will need at least twenty minutes of the team's time to discuss some important issues.
- During the meeting, if she attempts to take over the conversation say, "Yes, that is a very important issue, too, and I would like to discuss that after we finish the item that I brought up."
- Before the meeting respectfully tell her that you feel there has been lopsided attention in the meetings and you would like more time in the future.
- Confront your coworker right after a meeting where she monopolized and tell her how you feel about it.
- Confront your coworker in the meeting when she interrupts. Respectfully, ask her not to do it again.

I am not necessarily recommending any of the steps above, but rather I am demonstrating what a fear hierarchy might look like. This may or may not resemble a hierarchy for you. Some things that I have listed that might be more frightening than others to me may be less frightening than others for you. On your fear hierarchy there are no right answers, only your answers.

Once you build your hierarchy, then you start with the one that scares you the least. Once you master it, you then go on to the next one. It is important to realize that you might feel some fear each time you move up your hierarchy (that is only natural). This fear should be dealt with one step at a time. As you move up your hierarchy, your confidence will continue to grow, and eventually you will be desensitizing yourself to the fear. In our analogy of the swimming pool, you are the one-step-at-a-time person. Each step only occurs when you are "used to the water" and ready to face the next level.

Exercises
Self-reflection exercise: Build a fear hierarchy

Create your personal fear hierarchy. Remember that you can either use one situation with different levels of fear or build a hierarchy covering several different situations. Try to come up with ten steps if possible. Put the action that you fear the least as number one.

Self-challenge exercise: Start walking through your hierarchy mentally

Take a few minutes each day to close your eyes and imagine yourself doing the actions on your fear hierarchy. Try to imagine the action in every detail. Imagine what you would see, what you would hear, and what you would feel. Imagine yourself growing in confidence and ability as you walk through each of the actions. Keep doing this exercise daily until your fear diminishes enough to start doing the actions in reality.

Make a checkmark below for the days that you practice your imagery this week.

Mon   **Tues**   **Wed**   **Thurs**   **Fri**   **Sat**   **Sun**

Next steps and additional resources

Start doing your fear hierarchy. Take the least frightening step first. After you have accomplished that step, move on to the next step. If you find that you are too frightened to move to the next step, then you need to build more steps between the one that you accomplished and the one that you are avoiding. If this is the case, then redo your hierarchy and start walking through it again. Keep at it until you face the thing you fear most (of course, use your good common sense to make sure it is something that you should face).

For additional help in facing fear, try *Feel the Fear and Do it Anyway* by Susan Jeffers.

> *"Without courage, all other virtues lose their meaning."*
> —Winston Churchill

Chapter 7:

How to Make Conflict Less Frightening...Quickly

In the last chapter I used the analogy of getting into a cold swimming pool to talk about two distinct styles people have when it comes to facing fear. In that chapter we examined the step-at-a-time method. In this chapter we will look at the opposite style, a style that takes more initial courage, but that has faster results. We will look at the approach of diving into the cold water!

Real life

I had wanted to go on a cruise for years. I love the water, I love visiting places I have never been to before, and (sigh) I love buffets. Therefore, a cruise sounded perfect to me. So the family got tickets and we set off for the Western Caribbean. Our cruise stoped at Cozumel, Mexico; Jamaica; and the Grand Caymans. When we got settled on the boat there was a list of activities that we could choose from. One that immediately caught my eldest son's attention was an activity in Grand Cayman called "swim with the stingrays." Now, is it me, or does the title "swim with the sting (fill in the blank with anything you want)" not sound like a particularly good idea? Stinging is bad. Therefore, swimming with something that stings doesn't sound like the most intelligent thing to do while on vacation. However, my son was determined that we needed to experience this activity. On the brochure the words "safe" and "fun" were repeated frequently—and the people pictured did not look like they were in pain or needing hospitalization—so I agreed to sign the family up (knowing full well that the odds of getting my wife to jump in stingray-infested water was up there with the odds of winning the lotteries in every state, simultaneously).

When we arrived at Grand Cayman it was a beautiful day and we quickly boarded our little boat to head out to our fun activity. As we started getting close to the lair of the stingrays, our hosts passed out the informed consent forms we had to sign before getting our snorkeling equipment. Remember how the words "fun" and "safe" were prominently featured on the brochure? Well, the informed consent form highlighted different words. Interesting words, such as "illness" and "death," as well as multiple usages of the phrase "not responsible" were repeated frequently. I looked at my son, he looked at me, and we signed the forms. We just couldn't back out now. In addition, the captain of our vessel issued a challenge to us. "The hardest part is getting one of you to get in the water. Once one gets in, then the rest will follow. You can decide if you are brave enough to go in first." With that, my son looked at me with what I thought was courage in his eyes and raised his hand. I felt so proud that he was determined to prove his courage at such a tender age. I glanced around at the other tourists proudly thinking, "That's my boy," when Zach said five words that quickly changed my mood. He took his hand down, pointed at me, and loudly announced, "My dad will do it." You can imagine how my thought of "That's my boy" quickly shifted to "Wait until I get you in private." But it was too late. I was now offered up as the ceremonial stingray bait. I looked in Zach's eyes, and he said, "You can do it, Dad. You are going to be the first one in, right?" All of the sudden, the idea of a family cruise did not seem nearly as good of an idea as it had months earlier.

As we arrived in the area, all we could see was perfectly clear water that was about four feet deep with tan colored sand covering the entire area beneath the water. Our hosts explained that everyone would be fine as long as they did not step on the stingrays. I quickly ascertained that stepping on the stingrays was bad, so I was not going to plan to do that. I did not want to let my son down, so sure enough I was first in line to get in (grabbing him so that he would have to be next behind me). I thought, "This isn't that bad, I can do this, no sweat." Then it happened. Through this perfectly clear water glided a black monstrosity with a six foot wingspan. Then another, and another, until there were about fifty stingrays around the boat.

There was no way to get used to this fear in a step-by-step fashion. I had to back out or take the plunge. I took the plunge. As you can imagine, I was quite alert as the stingrays started swimming around me. I jumped when the first one touched me (slimy little buggers). Then I coaxed Zach to come in. He took the plunge too. However his plunge involved jumping on me and climbing up my back as far as he could so as to expose as little of his body as possible to the stingrays. As I struggled to steady myself in the water, I kept glancing down at my feet thinking, "Stepping on stingrays is bad. Stepping on stingrays is bad. Stepping on stingrays is bad." With my son screaming in my ear, I almost couldn't hear the other tourists slowly getting in and emitting screams every time a stingray came near. It was a scream fest. We were all out of our comfort zones and we did not feel safe.

However, a funny thing occurred. Eventually Zach got down in the water and he and I started wanting the stingrays to come by us. We wanted to pet them and stick our face under the water with goggles on so that we could see their faces. The crew of the boat even gave us squid to feed the stingrays, which caused them to surround us and eat right out of our hands. Soon all of the screams stopped (except when my wife shocked me by jumping in the water to get a quick picture with the stingray before fleeing to the boat again). People were having fun. Stingrays weren't nearly as scary as we thought. By plunging in, we quickly got used to them and were even disappointed when it was time to go. Both Zach and I loved the experience and we would do it again in a second.

How it applies

While swimming with stingrays is not a conflictual situation, it is a situation that demonstrates one way to deal with fear. This complex technique is well summed up in the old Nike slogan of "Just do it." Pretty simplistic, isn't it? And yet there is much wisdom to the technique of just doing it. Think about it. If you wait until you're not afraid before you face something, then you will likely never face it. However, if instead you just dive in and face it, then as long as there are no traumatic outcomes your fear will eventually decrease. All you have to do is keep doing the activity until your fear decreases. But you have to stay with it. If I had jumped out of the water before my fear of the stingrays had decreased, I would have reinforced the fear. Instead, I stayed in the water until my fear was eliminated, and then it actually turned to pleasure.

Most of the conflict cowards I have coached exaggerate the dangers of conflict. When they summon the courage to face it and keep at it persistently, they discover that much of the fear was caused by their imagination rather than reality. And even on those less frequent occasions when the other people involved in the conflict do not respond well, the outcome is bearable and not as crushing as previously believed. By persistently forcing themselves to face the conflict, they get over their fear much more quickly than people who have to deal with their fears more methodically.

This leaves you with a choice. Would you rather:

A) Take the route that has less initial pain, but takes longer, or

B) Take the route that is faster, but initially more painful

Again, there is no right answer, only your answer. If, however, you decide to dive in, you need two things: courage and tenacity. If you are that person who jumps into a cold swimming pool rather than walking slowly into the water, then you know that there is always a little fear before jumping in. However, you somehow summon the self-discipline to just make yourself jump in. Once in the cold water, you have to have the self-discipline to stay in the water until your body adjusts to it. If you get right out of the water, then all of your initial pain was in vain. Therefore, when dealing with a conflictual situation, if you don't have the self-control or discipline to stick with it, then you probably should take the step-by-step route. If, however, you are tenacious and dedicated to sticking it out, then diving in might be the right approach for you. Also, there are some times when you may choose the more methodical approach and other occasions where you decide that it is wise to take the plunge.

So follow these steps:

Step 1: Examine the situation and determine if it is appropriate to confront the problem.

Step 2: Make a choice between using our methodical step-by-step approach or the "just do it" method.

Step 3: If you choose to just do it and it is safe to do so, then do it.

Step 4: Keep with it until it is resolved or your fear has decreased significantly (as long as it continues to be wise to stay on course).

Step 5: When necessary (if the situation starts getting out of hand), agree with the other person involved to take a break in order for both of you to calm down and come at the situation in a way that is helpful. Agree to a specific time to address the problem to help keep both of you on track.

The Nike advertising campaign struck a cord in the American public. It touched on a truth that we know on a deep level. Sometimes you need to take your time and analyze a situation very methodically before attempting anything. Other times you need to "just do it."

Exercises
Self-reflection exercise: The pain and pleasure of just doing it
Remember our pain/pleasure method from chapter 5? With a slight variation we can use it to help you decide which method is right for you. Complete the following chart for a conflict situation you are currently facing. List the pain (or negatives) of using each approach and the pleasure (or positives) of using each approach. Use it to decide which method you want to use to handle the conflict:

	Pain	Pleasure
Use a step-by-step approach		
Use a just-do-it approach		

Self-reflection exercise: A "just do it" memory
Write out an example from the past when you decided to face your fear by "just doing it." Reflect on the pros and cons of taking that approach. Are you glad you did it? Would you do it differently if you could?

Next steps and additional resources

Look for a chance to "just do it" when it comes to a minor conflict experience. Notice how you feel afterwards. Examine how this approach works for you. Try to open your eyes to other situations where this approach might be preferred over the step-by-step method.

For anyone with intense fears and anxieties that seemed deeper than what we are discussing, try *The Anxiety and Phobia Workbook* by Edmund J. Bourne, Ph.D.

"The difference between a successful person and others is not a lack of strength, not a lack of knowledge, but rather a lack of will."

–Vince Lombardi

Chapter 8:

How Your Integrity Can Help You Face Conflict

Sometimes we need to examine the reactions that other people will have to our behavior before we decide if we are going to take action. Other times we need to do the right thing despite the consequences. When we fail to do the right thing, we experience more than the pain of the situation, but also a specific pain that can only be created by ourselves. The pain that no one else can cause us. Some might argue that it is the worst pain of all. What is the pain? It is the pain of self-betrayal. In this chapter we will look at how your personal integrity may play out in times of conflict.

Real life

Ed was an manager in a mid-sized company and a coaching client of mine. He had come to coaching because he knew that he wanted more fulfillment in his career. Through a series of exercises, questions, and experiences, Ed soon saw that he did love the company he worked for, but that his talents and desires were better suited for a different position. This other position would be a major promotion for him, and we set our sights on building a strategy to help him get this position. Within a short period of time, Ed had worked very hard and strategically, and indeed was one of the potential candidates for the promotion. He and I were both excited to see our work about to pay off in full. Then came the glitch.

Because of Ed's personality, people tended to open up to him quickly. During his interview with the CEO of the company, the CEO blurted out information about some hiring practices that were fairly standard for the company that tended to favor men over women for significant positions. This was shocking to Ed and completely betrayed Ed's personal beliefs about equality in the workplace. However, he was so caught off guard that he did not respond to the statement. Later, he phoned me and asked to have an extra telephone coaching session in order to process the situation.

He asked, "How can I confront the CEO about this? Not only will I probably lose the promotion, but I could lose my job."

With many of my clients, this fear might be irrational, but in Ed's case there was some evidence that suggested he was facing a true job threat. Through a series of coaching questions, I helped Ed look at the odds of the negative outcome happening as well as explore the possible positive consequences of having that discussion with the CEO. More importantly, however, Ed and I looked at the consequences to his own self-concept and respect if he *did not* say anything about these offending business practices. In the end, Ed decided that he had to do the right thing and accept whatever consequences came from his actions. We spent the rest of the phone call drafting up how he would confront the CEO to make sure it was respectful, not attacking, persuasive, and honest. In short, Ed knew what he had to do and he was going to do it, but he was going to make sure he did it well.

The next day Ed met with the CEO and explained with respect and honesty what he felt about the practice of favoring men for higher positions in the company. He ended his discussion with: "I thought you needed to know what you would be getting if you promoted me to this position. I would not show this favoritism and I would stand up to anyone who did show it. Because I respect you, I thought you had the right to know what I am about so that you can make the decision that serves our company best. I want this position, and if I get it I will do great things for this company, but I could not take the position without being honest with you. This promotion is very important to me, but my integrity is more important to me."

The surprised CEO leaned back in his chair, and there was silence in the room.

How it applies

Doing the right thing is not always easy. Sure it is easy if you will get praise and accolades for your action, but what about those times when there is a potential cost for you to honor what you really believe? That is a situation that separates those of us who claim to have integrity from those of us who don't. You may be reading this section questioning, "But what happen with Ed? Did he get fired? Was his boss mad? What happened?" The point is: *It does not matter how the boss reacted to Ed!* Either way, Ed was a winner because he was true to himself and his standards of conduct. The success of the story does not depend on what Ed's CEO did; the success of the story is solely based on what Ed did. Anything else is just a fringe benefit.

However, just to satisfy your potential curiosity, I will tell you what happened to Ed. He got the promotion. Not only did Ed get the promotion, but he gained the respect of that CEO. So much so that the CEO started asking more frequently for Ed's advice and perspective because he trusted Ed to "tell it like it is" rather than pacify him like so many of the other managers. Ed also had impact on the company as a whole. In time, more women were promoted to positions of greater responsibility, and favoritism was shown on the basis of skill and talent rather than gender. I talk to Ed every now and then. The last I heard, he had gotten another promotion and loved his career. He felt absolutely great about the impact he had on the CEO and the company as a whole.

I celebrate the fringe benefits that Ed received and I celebrate that his boss was able to look at himself and change, but again I want to emphasize that I would have celebrated with Ed even if he had been fired. His boss had the power to fire Ed, but he did not have the power to take away Ed's integrity. Only Ed has the power to betray himself. Only Ed could commit self-betrayal and live with that decision.

Have you ever betrayed your beliefs? I have, far too many times in my life. If they ever invent a reliable time machine I would love to go back in time and change my integrity failures. Since I will likely not have this option, I have to take my peace in trying to learn from my mistakes and in trying my best to do the right thing now even if it costs me. While I can point to many times when I have betrayed my integrity, I also can point to other times in my life where I maintained my integrity, in the face of difficult consequences. I don't regret any of these times when I stayed true to myself. Not a single one.

Do you have similar memories? Most of you will. Remember these memories on those occasions when you know you should face a conflict yet are tempted to avoid it. These memories will remind you that nothing is worth the cost of betraying yourself.

Exercises
Self-exploration exercise: Exploring your values

Make a list of those values that are most important to you (such as respecting others, honoring God, doing your best whenever possible, helping others, being authentic, etc.). After you have finished the list, rank them in order of importance to you. Then reflect on how you spend your time and money. Does your time match what you really value? Write a sentence or two about how your values play out in conflict situations.

Self-exploration exercise: Traveling back in time to make a change

Pick three events from the past where you betrayed your integrity in order to avoid a conflict. Write down what you wish you would have done differently. Then record what you learned from this experience that will help you not repeat it in the future. Finally, make sure you forgive yourself for being human and make a commitment to yourself to do better next time you are faced with a similar situation.

	Describe the situation	If you could go back in time, what would you do differently?	What did you learn from this past experience?
Past situation #1			
Past situation #2			
Past situation #3			

Next steps and additional resources

Examine your life currently. How true are you being to yourself? Where are you betraying something that you really believe in order to avoid a conflict? Consider the cost of continuing this act of self-betrayal and do something about it.

For information on living with integrity, try *The Road Less Traveled* and *Further Along the Road Less Traveled* by M. Scott Peck, M.D.

"Right is more precious than peace."

—Woodrow Wilson

"All honor's wounds are self-inflicted."

—Andrew Carnegie

"The man who views the world at fifty the same as he did at twenty has wasted thirty years of his life."

—Muhammad Ali

Chapter 9:

Understanding When Conflict Is Actually a Good Thing

Most of us think of conflict as a very negative experience. The truth is that without conflict we would not have close relationships. Without conflict we would likely be less motivated to do our best. Without conflict we would likely never change our minds about anything! In this chapter we will look at those occasions where conflict is helpful and positive.

Real life

When I was practicing therapy instead of coaching, I use to run men's groups. I absolutely loved facilitating these groups. I had always been a sensitive kid and wasn't athletic growing up. The combination of these two tendencies meant that I didn't hang around much with high testosterone individuals. Therefore, spending time with a group of people who were striving to be men of both strength and nurturance was a privilege for me.

Anyone who has ever worked with groups knows that groups tend to follow a specific series of developmental stages. One of the stages is often called "storming." This stage can be thought of as "the honeymoon is over" situation. Before this stage, the group members tend to be very supportive and caring. In the storming stage, individual differences create conflict and control battles. The men's group did not skip this stage.

Jeff was the heart of the group. He was an extremely sensitive man who had the potential to be incredibly loving and, on occasion, incredibly angry. He was soft-spoken, kind, and analytical. An intelligent man who had been hurt by too many people in his lifetime, Jeff tended to contain his feelings until they built up to an explosion. Dan, on the other hand, was a drama king.

Every emotion was worn on his sleeve. Every challenge was a crisis. And every insensitive word was a huge attack on his personage. On the positive side, Dan was the life of the party. You just enjoyed his presence. When he was happy, you were happy. When Dan was in a good mood, he was sucking every breath out of every moment of life. When he was in a bad mood, you wanted to head for the hills. Of course, the first day of group I predicted in my mind that these two men would be the first to irritate each other to the point of conflict.

One evening Jeff was sharing a particularly hurtful event from his week. Dan, in an attempt to help, gave Jeff his best, "you've got to make lemonade out of lemons" speech and challenged Jeff to quit feeling sorry for himself. Tick-tock, tick-tock, tick-tock, I looked over at Jeff and I knew that the explosion was coming fast. My first and most primal instinct was to quickly jump in and pacify Jeff. I wanted to communicate how Dan was attempting to help and gently ask Jeff what he needed from the group. In other words, my automatic desire was to head the conflict off at the pass. But, and this is a big but, I knew that if I interfered, then I would be trying to avoid the very stage necessary to help the group move to the next level of communication. So I used one of my best therapy skills—I kept my mouth shut.

Dan kept talking, completely oblivious to the veins popping out on Jeff's forehead. I think that Dan was about to jump into "when the going gets tough the tough get going" routine when Jeff exploded.

> Jeff: What are you, a complete moron?! You always do this! If I hear one more idiotic cliché from you, I'm going to throw up. Do you even listen to yourself?

> Dan: How can I possibly listen to myself with you whining all of the time? Get a grip on it, Jeff! The whole world doesn't center on what you think and feel. Quit feeling sorry for yourself and live a little!

Other group member's eyes got big as Jeff and Dan started escalating the volume and the criticism. It is always difficult as a group facilitator to know when to jump in. In this case, the cue was both Jeff and Dan jumping out of their chairs and heading for each other! I managed to leap out of my seat and got between them before they made contact. After a few calming words, I got them to sit back down in their seats and invited the group to process the interaction. I then turned to each of them and thanked them, saying:

"Gentlemen, we owe a debt to Jeff and Dan tonight. Conflict has to happen in every group or the group will stagnate and die. If there is no conflict then there is no genuineness or individuality. Now we have a choice. We can ignore the fact that we just had conflict, which will lead to shallow relationships. We can panic at the fact that we just had conflict, which will lead to people leaving the group and missing out on the growth possible here. We could be angry about the fact that we had conflict and decide not to trust each other or to be bitter, but that path leads to the death of these relationships. Or, we could accept the fact that we just had conflict, try to understand it, see where we made mistakes, and do our best to learn from it. Learn about ourselves and learn about each other. I invite you to take this last option. Now, what was happening in you, Jeff, and in you, Dan, that created this conflict?"

That night changed the group. After that, people were more authentic. If they said a kind word, you really believed them. You knew they weren't afraid of being honest with you. The men started seeing their differences as a strength of the group rather than a weakness. They were more intimate in sharing their feelings and more open to different perspectives. Jeff saw that there was some truth in what Dan said and Dan gained insight into how his approach was not always best for someone else. The two of them became good friends and to my knowledge are friends to this day.

How it applies

The conflict between Jeff and Dan could have ended very badly. It could have destroyed their relationship and even possibly the group. But it didn't. We utilized the conflict to improve the group and the relationships. Remember that this was a situation in which the conflict was not initially handled very well. In fact, it was handled very poorly. Just imagine, if we can achieve positive results when conflict is handled poorly, how much better can our outcomes be when we handle it well?

As mentioned earlier, there are many benefits to healthy conflict including:

- Better relationships
- Increased confidence
- Less anger and depression
- Greater respect from others
- Greater self-respect
- Increased intimacy
- Career enhancement (such as raises, promotions, easier days, etc.)
- Peace

Many times we forget about the benefits. Much of our perspective is related to how our family of origin handles conflict. When I look at my own family there is quite a difference between how different family members dealt with conflict.

A few years ago my grandmother passed away. "Nanny" Vance led an outstanding life. She was the most compassionate woman I ever met and she never had an unkind word to say about anyone. I never knew Nanny to ever be in conflict with anyone. I also never remember her being outspoken about her opinions. However, the same couldn't have been said for my grandfather. Although he died when I was nine, his legacy was one of a somewhat critical man who you did not want to cross. From what I have been told, you always knew where he stood and you risked humiliation if you did not take the same position on an issue (although as family history is often tainted, it is possible that this was not the reality of who he was, but I can only operate on limited memory in this case). My mother is definitely more like her mother. You can pretty much count on her smoothing (or attempting to smooth) out things between siblings before anyone has a chance to speak a harsh word. She just wants everyone to get along.

My father's parents were exactly the opposite. Papa was a worker in the steel mills, but soft-spoken, kind, and loving. You could always count on a scruffy kiss with a hint of aftershave from him when you greeted him at the door. Again, I never saw him in conflict with anyone. His wife, Mama, was a complete fireball. She was from the back hills of Kentucky and you *did not* want to be on her bad list. She would tell me stories of beating up women who looked at my grandfather "the wrong way" when they were dating. She was a hard woman who knew how to hold her own. My father was definitely more like his mother than Papa. It seemed like he always had a crusade against someone or something. He was a passionate man who could be very loving, and then at other times be very critical and aggressive.

I share my family legacy to help explain why I was such a coward when it came to conflict. I saw two styles of dealing with conflict. You either stay passive or you get loud and destructive. I chose to stay quiet. It seemed safer and not as ugly. So I was one of those people who avoided conflict, stuffed my feelings, and developed stomach problems by an early age.

I wasn't exposed to the benefits of conflict growing up, and it took my own experiences as an adult to change my perspective. It is probably why there is always a "little Timmy" inside who dislikes conflict. But fortunately the adult Tim has grown to understand that conflict, when handled well, can be a powerful force for change and for intimacy.

Exercises
Self-reflection exercise: Your family legacy
Write one or two sentences below that describe how each person in your family handled or handles conflict. Include stepparents and other important relatives, as you deem necessary.

Paternal grandfather:

Paternal grandmother:

Maternal grandfather:

Maternal grandmother:

Father:

Mother:

Siblings (list a sentence for each):

Others:

How has this legacy of conflict behavior impacted you? Do you choose to continue the legacy or to change it?

Self-reflection exercise: Learn from your own past

Write down a narrative of a past experience that you had with conflict that had positive results. Then create one sentence that reflects what you learned from the experience.

Now, pick a conflictual event from the past that did not go well (and you believe that it could have gone better). Explore in writing what you could have done differently that could have increased the odds of the conflict going well. Use this insight to learn for the future. Also examine if there is anything that you could still do about this past situation. If there is anything to do, then do it! If not, then work to let it go and focus on the things that you can impact now.

Self-reflection exercise: What is your perspective?

Write down every positive word and phrase that you can think of related to conflict. Try to come up with at least twenty words or phrases.

Next steps and additional resources

Take your list of positive phrases and words related to conflict and put them on a sticky note. Put this note someplace where you can see it every day, such as your computer screen or your mirror at home. When you face a potential conflict, remember all of the great things that could come from working through the conflict well.

To better understand how your childhood has impacted how you emotionally handle conflict and other aspects of life, try *Homecoming* by John Bradshaw.

> *"Coming together is a beginning; keeping together is progress; working together is success."*
>
> —Henry Ford

Chapter 10:

Building Your Knowledge, Skills, and Confidence

At times people avoid conflict simply because they have not developed the knowledge, skills, and thus the confidence for handling difficult situations. In this chapter I will emphasize the role of each of these in building your ability to deal with conflict.

Real life

Tonya was a senior manager in a high tech company in Texas. I have never met her, but we worked together for about six months over the phone. She had been promoted several times because of her uncanny ability to produce results. Unfortunately, her managerial skills did not match her technical skills, and she found herself in somewhat of a dilemma. She was in charge of motivating a team of highly individualized people. Each team member was highly qualified in technical skills, but they had never worked together before. Therefore, they got off to a rocky start. Tonya complained to me that she had given them clear directions concerning the goals of the joint project, but that the interpersonal differences were interfering with the team achieving the results that she had hoped they could achieve. She was baffled on what to do next.

Tonya was not naïve. She was extremely intelligent and quite capable in her field. However, in the field of human psychology she had much to learn. As we began our relationship Tonya asked me to train her in team-building, communication, and motivation skills. In time she came to understand conflict situations and gained much insight into how to motivate a team to work through conflict in a healthy manner. She was a fact-learner and implemented ideas quickly and effectively.

Tonya calls in for booster sessions every quarter or so, but for the most part she has been able to develop highly effective team members who perform great as individuals, but who can also maximize their efforts by working together.

How it applies

Tonya did not have an inability to deal with conflict; she just had never been taught an effective way to handle differences. Her block to success was more intellectual than emotional. She just needed to understand techniques that would improve her ability to handle problem situations and differences of opinion. Once she understood the techniques, she applied them like she applied all of her other knowledge, quickly and efficiently. People like Tonya need knowledge and techniques before they feel comfortable tackling a problematic situation.

How much of your conflict avoidance is due to confusion about how to handle the challenge of conflicts? If you are mainly struggling with a lack of knowledge, then you are in luck. In the upcoming chapters we will deal specifically with concrete and proven techniques for handling conflict.

Stephen Covey, the author of *The Seven Habits of Highly Successful People,* claims that we need three things in order to create behavior change—motivation, knowledge, and skills. My goal in the pages leading up to this has been to help build your motivation. I want you to realize that you are not the only person out there who has had to struggle with facing conflict. I also want you to fully consider the reasons that you want to change your conflict style. Hopefully, you now feel an even stronger commitment to learn how to effectively face conflict. In the next section of this book we will be focusing on knowledge. Chapters 11 through 19 explore common reasons for conflict. Gaining knowledge about what causes conflict gives us a more strategic way of looking at how to deal with the conflict. Starting in chapter 20 we will shift our focus to actual concrete techniques and skills, so that by the time you are done with this book you will be ready to take on anything that *you choose* to take on.

Exercises
Self-reflection exercise: Strengths and weaknesses
What conflict resolution skills do you already have that could be helpful as you grow to deal with conflict more directly (e.g., honesty, persuasiveness, etc.)?

What conflict resolution skills do you feel you need to gain?

Besides this book, what other resources do you have that could help you improve your ability to handle conflict effectively?

Next steps and additional resources
If your motivation to face conflict has not grown from reading the initial chapters of this book, then go back and start over. This time put even more effort into the exercises. Ask for help from a good friend who could support you in this journey.

For added insights into the role of knowledge, skill, and motivation in changing behavior, try *The Seven Habits of Highly Effective People* by Stephen Covey.

If your motivation is high and you are ready to learn more, then what are you waiting for? It is time for the next section!

"Failure to prepare is preparing for failure."

—John Wooden

Section III:

Common Causes
of Conflict

Chapter 11:

We'd Be Fine if
They Weren't So Different!

Personality differences are one of the main reasons people get into conflict. While personality theory is beyond the scope of this book, we will explore common behavior patterns (ways that we prefer to act and behave). These preferences form habit patterns that can often make us fairly predictable in our actions. These differences in style lead to great conflict when we forget that there are often many valid ways to react to a situation. Many times, conflict is just due to differences in how we prefer to see and interact with the world. In this chapter we will explore one system for measuring and learning to adapt to different behavioral styles. Understanding these differences can keep the conflict healthy or even prevent unnecessary conflict from occurring.

Real life
Read each of the following stories and examine how behavioral styles may be involved.

You say tomato. I say, "You're wrong."
Randy and Sarah have been working together for two years. Randy is the ultimate in organization and efficiency. He has trouble concentrating when his desk is not in order or when he sees something amiss in his office space. Only after a thorough organizing of his office does he feel at peace. He likes to label his in and out file stacks according to the level of priority. If he had the time, he probably wouldn't mind organizing all of his desk contents in alphabetical order in order to be able to find his paper clips, pens, etc., with greater efficiency. Sarah is the opposite; messes and disorganization do not bother her

a bit. In fact, Sarah likes the freedom of not having to worry about organization. She has her own unusual system for finding things and does not like to be constrained by rigid organization. Oh sure, there are many times it takes her a little longer to find things and some objects get misplaced, but she sees that as a small price to pay for the freedom her lifestyle gives her. Randy and Sarah drive each other crazy in the workplace.

Interestingly, when working on a project together, their tendencies become even more pronounced. Randy shows more of a need for order than usual, and Sarah seems more disorganized than ever. In addition, each becomes more adamant than ever that their way is the right way. Randy sees Sarah as undisciplined. Sarah views Randy as obsessive. Both try to champion their way to the other only to have their coworker become more deeply entrenched in his or her original stance. Sarah is fearful that if she gives in and tries to be more organized, then she will lose freedom and Randy will expect even more from her. Randy is fearful that if he does not continue to push Sarah about being more organized, then their projects will be sloppy and second-rate. What neither realizes is that the taking of an extreme position actually acts as a catalyst for the other person to become more extreme. Also, they are so busy reacting to each other that they have forgotten what they truly feel and believe. Accusations of, "You always have to have things perfect!" and, "You never know where information is when I need it!" have left them feeling disrespected by each other. Each is convinced that the other despises being on the team.

We were perfect parents.

Chicago is well-known for its freezing winters with lots of snow. Every winter, my wife and I wonder if we are insane to live in the Midwest, but it does have one great fringe benefit—sledding! I have always loved sledding, so I was very excited to take my then five-year-old son Zach out to a local sledding hill. After putting him in one of those adorable snowsuits that make children look like stand-ins for the Pillsbury Doughboy, we embarked on our journey to the sledding hill. It was a perfect day for sledding. We had several inches of snow covering the ground, and I couldn't wait to send Zach down that first hill. After pulling into the parking lot, I got out and grabbed the sled from the trunk. Zach was walking around the car just staring at the ground with a concerned look that I had seen often on this small boy's face. "We need to go home and get a shovel," he said. "What do you mean we need to get a shovel, honey?" was my response, as I was completely clueless to what he had conjured up in his little mind. "Daddy, we need to get a shovel so we can shovel the snow and see if we are in the lines." It was then that I realized that Zach was concerned because, given the inches of white snow on the parking lot, there was no way to tell if we were parked between the yellow stripes. Of course, we were the *only* car in a lot with two hundred parking spaces, but that did not carry weight with Zach.

To Zach, knowing where the lines are is essential. It is just the way he thinks. Being between the lines is important. In fact, it is crucial! Whenever we would go to a swimming pool, as most kids were running and jumping in the water, Zach would be at the rule board, studying and memorizing. Of course, he was always kind enough to let his parents know if we were breaking any of the rules. He preferred to know the structure that he would be operating in before playing. Out of great pride, my wife and I initially attributed his incredible obedience to our obviously superior parenting skills. We now believe that our pride was God's cue that we needed some humility. So in His infinite wisdom he gave us another child. Our second son, Colton, is a spitfire. He has a contagious passion for life and is often the life of the party. His joy truly knows no bounds. However, to him, "No" means "As a parent I am particularly proud that you have learned how to stick your finger in the electrical socket, please keep it up." Colton does not see lines in the same way Zach views them. To Colton, lines are an annoyance. Lines only serve to dampen his creativity and fun. To Zach, lines are comfort. To Colton, lines are constraints. They have two very unique styles. As I write this, God has again blessed us with a third son, Vance. I can't wait to see what He is trying to teach us this time.

You are going to be a success whether you like it or not.

Jeff was frustrated with his new employee. Michelle was an extremely talented individual who had impressed Jeff from their very first meeting. Jeff prided himself on being a powerful mentor. In fact, several of the people whom Jeff had managed had become superstars in the company. At recognition meetings,

Jeff would often be mentioned as someone who was critical to other's progress and success in the company. Jeff had great expectations for Michelle when she joined his team, but she had not lived up to those expectations. Michelle did excellent work and was highly valued on the team, but every time that Jeff started prodding her on her vision for the future in the company, he was met with what appeared to be disinterest. Unbelievably, Michelle seemed to be content with her current position and duties, and showed no interest for anything more. This made no sense to Jeff, who saw Michelle's potential as being much greater in his mind than what was demanded from her in her current position. In fact, he believed that if Michelle stayed in her current position, then she was squandering her potential and cheating the company. In their individual meetings he never failed to remind her that she was capable of much greater impact than what she could achieve in her current position. Whenever Michelle showed disinterest in moving up in the company, Jeff would pull out all stops to try to convince her why this was a mistake. He did this because he truly believed that this was the best way to help her.

Eventually, Michelle would make some statement of agreement that she should consider taking on greater responsibility, but her behavior following their meetings never indicated that she really wanted to change. Jeff just couldn't understand the way she thought about life and goals. He began to lose respect for her. The day that Michelle started talking about moving to a half-time position in order to start a family was the straw that broke the camel's back for Jeff. In complete confusion, he finally told Michelle that he just didn't understand her and wanted her to explain to him what she really wanted out of her job. Although somewhat hesitant, Michelle explained to him that security, stability, and predictability in her life were all much more important to her than things like "moving up the corporate ladder," "going to the next level," "taking your goals to the limit," or even making more money. She sheepishly added that she was feeling very pressured by him to become something that she didn't want to become, and that she had been thinking of finding a different job. Jeff was stunned. He wasn't trying to do anything wrong. He was just trying to mentor Michelle in the same way that he had mentored the "go-getters" that came before her. In his mind, he went back and forth in how he perceived the discussion that they were having. On one hand he thought that perhaps he had been wrong and owed Michelle an apology. On the other hand, he started wondering if she just had confidence issues and began to strategize on how he would help her work through these issues.

How it applies

In the above scenarios, we see some major differences in individual views and reactions to each other. We all have specific behavioral differences that impact all areas of our lives. There is bound to be conflict when people approach life so differently. After all, don't we tend to approach life in the way that we think is best? Therefore, if someone does it differently than we do, we will often label their way as bad, wrong, or less enlightened.

In our first example above, Randy and Sarah are quite different. However, Randy could likely learn some important things from Sarah, such as how to live more spontaneously and with more passion. Sarah, in contrast, could learn a lot from Randy about organization and planning. Unfortunately, if they never learn that they can actually benefit from their differences, they will likely drive each other crazy.

In the example of my sons, I hope you could see that I do not particularly value one son's tendencies over that of the other. Like Colton, I believe that it is a wonderful perspective to see beyond the lines, to have passion as a leading force in your life. I like creativity and thinking differently than the crowd. Like Zach, I know that sometimes you do need to draw within the lines to create a beautiful picture. Rules are helpful to us and we can be much more efficient at times by following procedures and sticking to proven systems. Basically, Zach can learn from Colton's passion, and Colton can learn from Zach's discipline. I can learn from both of them.

In the third example, we again have coworkers who do not get along well. This time, however, one of them manages the other, so there is a difference in power. This creates all sorts of potentially negative dynamics in the workplace. Jeff had a natural focus on drive, progress, and growth. He put far less value on predictability, and stability. Michelle had a natural focus on security, stability, and predictability and was less concerned with moving up the corporate ladder. Who was a better person? Who was a greater asset to the workplace? Who was right and who was wrong? The answer of course is that both of their styles have great value, and there is room in this world for us to have differences like Jeff and Michelle.

Understanding a person's behavioral type helps us relate to them better. It helps us realize that sometimes conflicts are due to simple differences rather than malicious purposes. There are many behavioral type indicators or tests that label different traits. In terms of combining simplicity and practicality, I favor a system called DISC. The DISC is based on psychologist William Marston's work on understanding the emotions of normal people. Knowing a colleague, friend, or spouse's preferred style on the DISC can help eliminate frustrations and increase your ability to communicate well with them. The DISC gives insight into how we tend to see and interact with the world.

The DISC system separates individuals into four main behavioral styles. Many different companies use many different terms to describe the styles. I prefer the terms dominance, influence, steadiness, and conscientiousness. Marsten's theory is beyond the scope of this book, so I will focus on ways to read a style rather than the theory behind the styles. A fairly easy way I use to differentiate the styles is to read people on two continuums: approach and focus of attention. When I refer to "approach," I am referring to how the individual processes information. Do they tend to think through things and act quickly or are they more systematic and methodical in their thinking and action? Obviously, two people exhibiting these extremes of approach might have difficulty getting along with each other. One person would be trying to speed up the conversation or situation, and one would be trying to slow it down and be more analytical in the discussion. So differences in approach could potentially lead to arguments or misunderstandings.

The second factor for differentiating the behavioral styles has to do with how people differ in their focus of attention. On a continuum, you can meet extremes of individuals who tend to focus on tasks and results, and people who tend to focus on other people and relationships. People who focus on results like to get things done. It gives them a sense of accomplishment. People who are at the other extreme on this continuum prefer focusing on relationships rather than tasks. Sometimes this can lead to conflict because these two extremes don't always see things the same way. By taking both styles of approach (fast or methodical) and focus of attention (tasks or relationships) we can come up with the four main behavior styles of dominance, influence, steadiness, and conscientiousness.

The DISC System

	Fast approach	Methodical approach
Focus on tasks	Dominance	Conscientiousness
Focus on relationships	Influence	Steadiness

Individuals who show a high dominance style are movers and shakers. They process information quickly and are focused on tasks. People high in dominance tend to be results-oriented, focused on challenge and power, and like to make decisions quickly and with confidence. They are the team members who you know will get the job done. They are often motivated by challenge, opportunity for achievements, and freedom from control.

People high in influence also process information quickly, but they tend to be more focused on relationships and people than on tasks. High influence individuals tend to be enthusiastic, charismatic, and like impacting other people. They are the team members who keep things exciting and everyone motivated. They are often motivated by recognition, relationships, and freedom from details.

Individuals who show a high steadiness style tend to process things more methodically than high dominance and high influence people. They are like the high influence people in that they tend to focus on people and relationships more than on tasks. High steadiness individuals tend to be loyal, cooperative, calm, and methodical in how they deal with life. They are the team members who make sure that everyone on the team is doing OK. They are often motivated by security, stability, and sincere appreciation.

The final of the four styles is high conscientiousness. Individuals high in conscientiousness are similar to the high steadiness people in that they like a more methodical approach to life, but are similar to the high dominance people in that they focus more on tasks than on people. High conscientiousness individuals tend to be analytical and precise, and value quality and accuracy on a project. They are the team members who keep standards high and pay attention to details. They are often motivated by professional standards, defined expectations, and a quality focus.

Obviously, not all of us fit completely in one of the four styles. You may have a mix of two of the styles. We all have a little of each inside of us, but we usually have a primary and secondary preference. In addition, our preferences may change. For example, my highest score is dominance when I am running my company. In contrast, my high influence comes out much more when I am at home. When I am coaching, I try to pull out whatever style best serves my client. To be successful in work and relationships, the real key is to be able to accept all four styles and have the ability to bring each out of ourselves and/or adapt to other people who show a different style. Some humorous examples help spell out the differences in the four styles even further.

The elevator

You are with a large group of people waiting for an elevator and the doors finally open up.

If you are high in dominance, you step into the elevator and push the "close door" button.

If you are high in influence, you step in the elevator and say, "Come on, there's room for everyone!"

If you are high in steadiness, you let everyone step in and you wait for the next elevator.

If you are high in conscientiousness, you step in, size up everyone, and then look at the weight limit charts on the elevator.

The speeding ticket

You are pulled over by the police officer for speeding.

If you are high in dominance, you step out of your car and argue with the officer (he obviously doesn't realize that you need to get somewhere and you don't have time for this).

If you are high in influence, you become your charming best and the officer leaves, thinking that you are best friends now.

If you are high in steadiness, you thank the officer for the ticket and may point out to her that you also were not wearing your seatbelt (just in case she didn't notice).

If you are high in conscientiousness, you politely pull out the "rules of the road" catalog and start preparing your logical defense.

While these are a little exaggerated, they do represent certain tendencies of each of the different styles.

Strengths and challenges of different styles

Differences in style can play out in relationships, and each style has its own set of strengths and challenges. People high in dominance need to watch being too directive, impatient, or insensitive, as they can sometimes steamroll over people in order to get the quick results they want. They may see themselves as effective and honest while others may view them as uncaring and pushy. People high in dominance are successful in getting along with other styles when they develop greater patience and tone down the intensity of their directness. On the other hand, people high in dominance have great strengths, including honesty, effectiveness, and leadership. If you want to tackle a tough job then you will want someone high in dominance on your team. They can often be fearless in the face of conflict and, in fact, often love the challenge. High dominance often brings with it great confidence and the ability to make things happen.

Individuals high in influence also have a specific set of strengths and weaknesses. These individuals need to be cautious that they don't try to gloss over tough problems with simple answers. They also have a tendency to over-promise and under-deliver (their excitement gets the best of them and they have good intentions, but may lack the discipline to follow through). High influence individuals also need to pay more attention to detail, since they often find the small details mundane and a nuisance. They are successful in getting along with others when they attend to true needs and issues, are specific in their approach, and improve their organizational skills. But let's not forget the strengths shown by high influence individuals. They have great passion for life and relationships. They are excellent at persuading and motivating people. If you want someone to energize your team, then the high influence individual is a great asset. In conflict they can be great at negotiating and keeping the process lively. High influence often brings with it much joy and energy for living.

High steadiness individuals are much more subtle in their challenges. They need to watch indecisiveness, being too indirect, and subconsciously discouraging others from change (because of their desire to keeps things "normal"). High steadiness people need to learn to be more direct and honest with what they think and feel. They benefit from being willing to look at change and adapt more quickly to it. And they grow when they realize that conflict is not necessarily a bad thing. They may see themselves as easy-going, but others may view them as wimps. High steadiness individuals do well when they become more assertive and direct, cope better with change, and learn not to take on everyone else's problem as their own. But again, let's not focus on their challenges at the expense of overlooking their wonderful strengths. High steadiness people are kind, giving, and loyal. They are very focused on trying to help everyone be comfortable in difficult situations. If you are in conflict and you need someone as a listening ear and a loyal supporter, then you want someone high in steadiness. High steadiness brings with it great assistance and devotion.

High conscientiousness individuals sometimes suffer from being overly perfectionistic. Peers may misinterpret their analytical nature by perceiving them as aloof or disinterested. At times, they can discourage creativity in others. High conscientiousness people need to learn to be more accepting of differences and realize that their way is not always the right way. They do well when they take more time to build relationships and work at being more encouraging of others. One of the best things individuals high in conscientiousness can do to minimize conflict is to increase their flexibility, since at times they are quite rigid in their view of the world. In terms of strengths, high conscientiousness individuals have many. If you want someone on your team who will maintain top quality standards, then you know who to pick! They are fantastic at being alert to details others might miss, and they deeply care about doing work that will represent them well. In conflict, high conscientiousness individuals can do a great job at taking the dramatic emotions out of the discussion and focus on problem-solving the issue at hand.

What happens in stressful or conflictual times?

While I believe that all people are unique and that none of us are completely predictable, we can look at some generalities with each style. Under high stress, dominance individuals can become dominating and controlling. Influence people can become manipulative and overly emotional. Steadiness persons can become passive and give in to others too easily. Finally, conscientiousness individuals can become paralyzed by their perfectionism and high expectations. These tendencies have a powerful impact on situations of conflict. Imagine putting four people in a room with a problem to solve, and one is dominating, one is manipulative, one is passive, and one is overly perfectionistic. Does that sound like a recipe for success to you? This is why so many organizations use my company to teach their employees the DISC. They know that the cost of not attending to personality differences is much higher than investing in the training.

The exciting thing for you as the reader is that if you understand these differences then you can "normalize" a conflict with someone. I'm using the psychobabble term "normalize" to refer to making something OK and normal rather than wrong and abnormal. For example, if you are high in dominance and your spouse is high is steadiness, then you will have some common discussions such as:

> *Dominance: You wouldn't believe my secretary today. I was trying to get to an important meeting that I was late for and she kept trying to ask me questions as I was heading out the door. Maybe I should can her and get someone more effective.*

> Steadiness: Oh, honey. I'm sure that she wasn't trying to make you late. I hope you weren't curt with her. Remember that she has a family to support.

Or maybe it looks more like this:

> *Steadiness: My sister asked me to watch her kids again Friday and I just didn't think that I could say no.*

> Dominance: You know, she really takes advantage of us. When was the last time she watched our kids? There are some things we need to get done around the house Friday. I'm calling to cancel.

Now, the exact nature of the discussion may differ, but the "feel" of the dialogue should be recognizable. Or let's imagine that you own a small business with someone else. If you are high in influence and your partner is high in conscientiousness, then you might experience many discussions like this:

> *Influence: You know, it wouldn't kill you to be a little friendlier to the customers in the store. We want them to enjoy coming here and see that we have a fun environment.*

> Conscientiousness: What are you talking about? I said hello when they came in. I don't want to be phony with them.

Or maybe sometimes it looks like this:

> *Conscientiousness: You have to keep better track of your expenses. How long has it been since you turned in an expense report?*

> Influence: Hey, I always get it in eventually. It will all work out. Quit worrying.

Again, the content of the exact discussion may change, but often the essence of the discussion remains the same.

These are common discussions that people of different styles have because they tend to think differently about the world. In the above examples you can tell when someone is interested in the task and when someone is interested in the person. If you could hear the tone in the discussion, you would recognize one as fast and one as more methodical. There is nothing wrong with these discussions. However, they do demonstrate differences that need to be discussed and worked through by problem-solving together. As stated at the beginning of this chapter, differences in behavioral style can often be the source of unneeded conflict. However, if you can recognize these differences and talk about them as normal and OK, then all people involved will be less defensive and will work harder to problem-solve together. In contrast, if you treat these differences as right and wrong, then your chances of resolving your conflict in a healthy way are greatly diminished.

Exercises
Self-reflection exercise: What is your style?

Use the informal assessment below to see which basic style fits you best. Please note that unlike an official DISC assessment, this self-assessment is not standardized. However, it should help you at least get a sense of your main style.

Beneath the names of the different styles are clusters of words. Think of a specific environment (such as work or home) and circle all of the words that you think describe how you act most of the time.

Dominance
Wants immediate results
Action-oriented
Makes quick decisions
Likes to solve problems
Desires power and authority
Very direct
Thrives on challenge

Influence
Likes group participation
Entertaining
Motivational
Generates enthusiasm
Desires to impact others
Views others optimistically
Loves being the center of attention

Steadiness
Consistent
Predictable
Stable
Good listener
Patient
Desire harmony in environment

Conscientiousness
Focuses on details
Checks for accuracy
Analytical
Systematic approach to work
Weighs plus and minus options
Desires for accuracy and standards

Likes a predictable routine   Likes being the expert

Dislikes conflict   Reserved and professional

Given the number of words you circled above and your own insight into your behaviors, circle which style likely describes you best:

Dominance   Influence   Steadiness   Conscientiousness

Self-reflection questions: What is the impact of your style?

Given your preferred style, what kinds of potential conflicts might you have with each of the other styles?

Dominance:

Influence:

Steadiness:

Conscientiousness:

Which of the above styles do you think will be the most difficult for you to deal with and why?

Interacting with others exercise: Who are you in conflict with now?

Think of someone you are currently having a problem with who has a different preferred style than you. Then do the following exercise (you can guess their style from the list of words above or by thinking about their approach and if they focus more on tasks or people):

Person's initials: _____   Person's suspected main style: _____

How might your differences in style be impacting how you interact?

What can you do to switch how you think about this person's style?

What can you do to adapt your behavior to this person that would help impact the situation?

How can you communicate with this person most effectively?

How can you utilize the strengths of this person's style in the situation with which you are dealing?

Next steps and additional resources

The best way to really learn this information on styles is to share your learning with someone else in your life. Ask them to give you feedback on which style they think best describes you. If their answers are different than yours, analyze what this difference may suggest. Remember that you may have a different preferred style in different environments, so take that into account when you are receiving that feedback.

If you are in conflict with someone, try experimenting with shifting your style to one that may serve him better. Analyze his response to your shifts. You may even want to discuss the shift that you are making with him.

If you would like to take a standardized DISC evaluation you can order a fully self-contained profile using our contact information from the back of this book. We also have an instrument that assesses two people on their DISC style, which we have used when coaching couples or partners. This fully self-contained instrument allows you to assess your own style while your partner assesses his. The booklet then walks you through conflict areas for each style and gives strategies for getting along better with others.

For other angles on Marsten's theory, try *The Platinum Rule* by Tony Alessandra, Ph.D. and Michael J. O'Connor, Ph.D. or *I'm Stuck, You're Stuck* by Tim Ritchey and Alan Axelrod. Finally, if you are interested in studying the background of the DISC theory, go to the library and find William Marston's *Emotions of Normal People*.

> *"If everyone is thinking alike then somebody isn't thinking."*
> —George S. Patton

Chapter 12:

Why People Only Think That They're Angry (Often They're Not!)

What emotion most often occurs in conflict? If your immediate answer was "anger," then you are both right and wrong at the same time. You are correct in that we frequently see anger when in conflict. However, a person who looks angry often is really feeling a different emotion. Frequently people are completely unaware of what they are feeling beneath the anger that they only *think they feel*. In this chapter we will look at the role of anger in causing conflict and how discovering your real emotions can often aid you in resolving differences.

Real life

Rick came into my office after having a terrible argument with his business partner, who also happened to be his sister. "She's a complete jerk!" was how he started off the conversation. He continued, "She always has to have things her way. Nothing anyone else does is ever good enough for her. She is totally anal-retentive. I mean, you would think that the world caved in just because we spent more money than she thought we should. I am sick and tired of having to deal with her attitude. Maybe it is time for me to get out of this business and start something on my own. Dad would be sick if he were alive to see what she does. It is pathetic."

I let Rick vent for a little while longer until he seemed spent. "Rick, what happened that got you so upset?" I asked. He went on to tell me about the months he spent planning a surprise birthday party for his sister at the office and his anger at her response to the party.

Rick attacked the party plans with gusto, investing a lot of company time and money into the extravaganza. His sister was indeed surprised at the party, but seemed to show concern along with some of her enjoyment. When Rick asked her what was wrong, she asked him how much the party had cost. When he told her, she appeared upset. "You really shouldn't have spent that much. We have had a tough couple months in the business and that probably wasn't wise to do." Rick could not believe what he was hearing. He had sacrificed many hours to make this party successful and he had done it all for her, only to be criticized. "Can you believe she said that to me? How ungrateful can you be?" he said after relating the story to me. I replied by asking him what he was feeling. "How do you think I'm feeling? I'm furious and I told her so. I really let her have it for being so ungrateful about it," he said. He went on to tell me that she did not respond well to his anger and that they were not currently talking to each other.

"Rick, you are telling me that you are furious or angry with her. What are some other feelings that you have about her response?" I asked. In fact, I had to ask Rick this question several times before he finally answered the question. Rick answered, "Look, I could never please the old man either. It just seems like no matter how hard I try, I can't make her happy just like I couldn't make Dad happy. You want to know what I really feel? I feel hurt. I feel hurt that she didn't appreciate my work. I feel hurt that she didn't see that I did this because I love her and appreciate what she does for the company. I feel hurt because I just feel like I will never measure up in my family's eyes." Rick's spirit completely changed as he talked about his hurt. He went from a pumped up, angry version of a man who had experienced a huge injustice to a soft-spoken and tearful young man who just wanted his sister's appreciation and love.

As we talked further I found out that Rick had historically responded to these situations with anger, and that neither Rick's father nor his sister had ever responded well to that approach. I encouraged him to try to approach his sister again, but this time to share with her like he had shared with me. In other words, to talk about his hurt rather than his anger. Rick was very reluctant to do this because it felt so vulnerable and he feared that he would get hurt again. We did some coaching work to help him focus on doing the right thing no matter how his sister would react, and he was able to motivate himself to talk to his sister about his hurt. Through that conversation, some great healing began between the two of them. His sister apologized for her insensitivity, and Rick apologized for his angry response. They made agreements on how to handle unusual purchases in the business and defined individual freedoms versus decisions that needed both of them. Eventually, they were able to talk honestly about their father, and compared notes on how each of them felt that he favored the other. They became more than siblings, they became good friends. They also agreed to always talk about what they were really feeling and to look for other emotions that might be hidden when they thought that they were angry.

How it applies

Few people have the emotional discipline and maturity to respond to anger nondefensively. Most of us do not handle angry attacks well. However, many people are much better at responding to other emotions besides anger. Think about it. Is it harder to listen to friends when they attack you with anger or if they come to you expressing hurt feelings? Is it harder to listen when a loved one says he is furious with you or when he says that he felt embarrassed by something you had said? Is it harder to strive toward compromise with a coworker who vents at you that you are "never available" or one who says she feels frustrated by the fact she can't complete a project without your help and it has been hard to get your attention lately?

The bottom line is that if you are looking to get a defensive response from someone, then the best approach is to approach them with anger. It is just human nature to respond poorly to this type of approach. Don't get me wrong, some people will respond poorly if you approach them with any emotion. But overall, other emotions tend to trigger defensiveness less often than expressions of anger. For some reason, many people find it easier to express anger than softer emotions. This is especially true for men who often will share anger rather than admit to hurt feelings. We can feel many emotions beneath our anger. These include:

- Hurt
- Shame
- Embarrassment

- Frustration
- Fear
- Humiliation
- Sadness
- Confusion
- Helplessness

Anger is often a secondary emotion in response to these other emotions. Another way to say this is that anytime you think that you are angry, you are probably experiencing another emotion that is equally or more important to process than your anger. In addition to being more honest with ourselves about what we really feel, there is also the benefit of how others often will respond if we share these deeper feelings. Just monitor your own response to the following scenario. Imagine that a friend comes to you and says:

"I am angry at you!"

What feelings immediately pop up for you? How likely are you to respond with calm care versus cautiousness or defensiveness? Now imagine that same friend saying one of the following:

- "I feel hurt because of what you said."
- "I get afraid when you talk like that."
- "I am frustrated by what is going on here."

What feelings immediately pop up for you? How were they different from the feelings that you felt when someone said they were angry with you? You would probably be more willing to hear the person out without feeling the need to prepare your mental defense.

People cause unnecessary conflict by ignoring their primary emotions and responding with anger. When we learn to pinpoint what we are really feeling, we create less conflict. When we learn to help other people pinpoint their primary feelings, then we help diffuse the intensity of the conflict and greatly improve our chances for having a healthy and happy resolution to the issue.

Exercises
Self-reflection exercise: What is your primary emotion?

Think of a time you expressed anger to someone else, when in reflection, you probably felt a different primary emotion beneath the anger. Then answer the following questions:

What were your primary emotions or emotion? (Circle any that apply)

Hurt	Shame
Embarrassment	Frustration
Fear	Humiliation
Sadness	Confusion
Helplessness	

How would it have impacted your discussion had you shared your primary emotions instead of your anger?

Why did you show anger instead of your primary emotion?

What can you learn from this event?

Understanding others exercise: What is their primary emotion?

Think of a time when someone approached you in anger, but you suspect that he/she felt a different primary emotion beneath the anger. Then answer the following questions:

What do you think were his or her primary emotions or emotion? (Circle any that apply)

Hurt   Shame
Embarrassment   Frustration
Fear   Humiliation
Sadness   Confusion
Helplessness

How would it have impacted your discussion had the person shared their primary emotions with you instead of his or her anger?

What could you have said or done to have helped him or her get in touch with the primary emotions?

Next steps and additional resources

Be a scientist this week. Every time you notice anger, ask yourself what emotion is beneath the anger. Do this with friends, at work, and at home. Analyze movies, soap operas, and television shows. Television is notorious for showing people angry at each other when they really feel something else. Try to imagine how each of these situations would have played out had the people been more emotionally honest with themselves and others. Use this information as motivation to keep focused on your primary emotions and not falling into the anger trap.

For additional techniques for handling anger, try *Dr. Weisinger's Anger Work Out Book* by Hendrie Weisinger, Ph.D.

"You cannot shake hands with a clenched fist."
—Golda Meir

"It's hard to stay mad when there's so much beauty in the world. Sometimes I feel like I'm seeing it all at once and it's too much. My heart fills up like a balloon that's about to burst. And then I remember to relax, and stop trying to hold on to it. And then it flows through me like rain, and I can't feel anything, but gratitude...for every single moment of my stupid little life."

—Actor Kevin Spacey playing a character
reflecting on his life in *American Beauty*

Chapter 13:

Five Ways to Listen and Why People Don't Use Them

Everyone knows that we need to listen to others. Despite that knowledge, most people are still poor listeners. In fact, some research suggests that we screen out about 70 percent of what others say to us. One part of our listening challenge is that there are many different ways to listen to someone. Sometimes people want us to listen to them in one way and sometimes they want us to listen to them in another way. Conflict arises when we use the wrong listening style. In this chapter you will learn five different ways to listen to someone else and when to use which.

Real Life

Tom was a decent guy in every way imaginable. You could not ask for anyone who would treat you with greater integrity and care. As a financial advisor, Tom started coaching with me because he wanted to take his business to the next level. He had done well, but knew that he was only scratching the surface when it came to the success of his business. As is customary in a first coaching session, we discussed his work goals and his life balance. One of the assessment tools that I use in the first session is the Personal Balance Wheel, which is a popular tool among coaches. The instructions to the balance wheel ask individuals to circle the number that best represents their level of satisfaction in eight different areas of life (7 = Completely satisfied; 1 = Completely dissatisfied). They then are asked to connect the dots and imagine how their car would travel if the wheels were in that shape!

The Life Balance Wheel

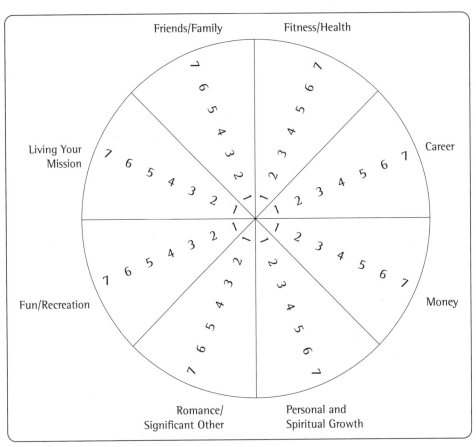

Tom was only dissatisfied with two areas on the balance wheel, "money" and "significant other." The money issue was one that we had already discussed. He basically wanted to make more income in order to retire early. He also had a philanthropic heart and had dreams of building a foundation that would help orphans. So, the score that he put under "money" was not a surprise. I had not, however, gotten any sense of dissatisfaction in his marriage. As I asked him about his relationship with his wife he mumbled something like, "She doesn't think I listen to her," but then made it very clear that he wanted to keep our discussion on the financial issues. In coaching, we honor where the client wants to go and do not force our own goals on them. Therefore, I dropped the subject and started analyzing his business practices with him.

I have worked with quite a few individuals in the financial services industry, and few impressed me as well as Tom. You could clearly see that Tom made decisions for his clients based on their needs and not his own. His clients had done well and most seemed pleased with his level of service and attention. Tom did all the right things in prospecting for clients and had many initial consultations. However, his prospect-to-client conversion ratio was much smaller than I would have suspected. Many of Tom's referrals came from current clients. Therefore, one of Tom's earliest coaching assignments was to follow up with the person that referred the prospect to him and see if they had any insight into why the person did not choose to use Tom's services. We picked a few of Tom's long-term clients with whom he felt comfortable asking for this feedback.

As we began this process, we noticed two trends in the feedback. Prospects who did not become clients were saying:

"I just didn't connect with him."
"He didn't seem to listen very well to what I was saying."

Tom was absolutely floored by the feedback. To be honest, I was somewhat surprised by it also. I knew that Tom cared about his clients, so what was the problem? Even more confusing was the fact that Tom's clients who were reporting this information back to us gave Tom the exact opposite feedback! They thought Tom was a fantastic listener and had absolutely no complaints about him. This aroused my curiosity greatly.

I decided to give Tom a few behavioral profiles that I often use with my coaching clients in order to unlock this feedback puzzle. One of the profiles that assesses listening styles gave us the key to this puzzle. Tom and I discussed five different ways of listening to others. No way is particularly right or wrong, but the insight that comes from the profile shows us that we need to be able to adapt to the right listening style in the right situation in order to be successful in any business connected to people and relationships. The five styles are:

- Appreciative listening
- Empathic listening
- Comprehensive listening
- Discerning listening
- Evaluative listening

I will describe the five styles of listening further in "how it applies," but for the sake of explaining Tom's challenge you need to know that he was completely lopsided on the evaluative listening scale. He was off the charts, so to speak, while none of the other four registered much of a blip on the radar screen. Evaluative listening in its most simplistic form is listening in order to fix something. This fix-it listening is great if that is what someone is looking for, but can be destructive when they want something different.

So here is what would happen. A new prospect would meet with Tom, and all of Tom's questions were geared to get the information he needed to recommend the best financial planning options for this prospect. The conversation was very task-oriented, and Tom's goal by the end of the meeting was to be able to "fix" the prospect's financial challenge. However, (and this is a *huge* however), some prospects were not looking for the fix. Some just wanted to get to know Tom to see if they could trust him. Some just wanted to share about their lives and dreams before they were "constrained" to a solution. Others were not ready to open up to Tom to give him the information he needed. They wanted to be less formal and more lighthearted. Tom was not listening in the way they wanted to be heard. Of course, the clients that referred the prospects *were* looking for evaluative listening, so they connected to Tom instantly. They wanted him to listen to them and gather information in a way that would fix their financial challenge. He had the right style for them.

This was a huge insight for Tom. He sat across from me and was quiet for the longest time. After long moments of silence, he finally said, "So, this is what she was talking about."

> TIM: I'm sorry Tom, what who was talking about?

TOM: Uh, my wife. She has always complained that I never listen to her. It never made sense to me. I listen to her all the time.

TIM: *How were you listening to her?*

TOM: I just wanted to help her. I love her so much, so whenever she had a problem, I wanted to make it better. It always frustrated me that she couldn't see I was trying to help her.

TIM: *Sounds like you are wondering if she really wanted you to fix the problem.*

TOM: Yep, I'm thinking that maybe that was the last thing she wanted me to do.

TIM: *What do you think she wanted you to do instead?*

TOM: I think that it goes back to one of the other styles. I think that she just wants me to empathize with what she feels.

TIM: *Do you want to explore what that might look like?*

TOM: That would probably be a good idea. She told me last week that she was considering leaving me.

That conversation was a huge breakthrough for Tom. With additional coaching and practice, he learned how to use the right style of listening for the right situation. Within six months, his prospect-to-client conversion rate doubled. Within two months, I received a thank you card from his wife. They were able to improve their relationship and both learned to listen to each other in the way that they needed to be heard.

Tom was not a bad man. Tom was not an uncaring man. Tom was not a man who did not listen to others. Tom was a man who had a habit of listening in only one way. Once he realized this and changed his habit, all of his true care and listening were evident to those around him. They were happier, he was more effective, and we hit our goals for coaching, both financial and personal. He had less conflict in his life once he learned how to listen to people in the way they needed to be heard.

How it applies

There are several points that we can take from the above story concerning conflict:

- Conflict is not always intentional (Tom did not mean to be listening with the wrong style).
- Conflict is not always dramatic. (One could argue that there was conflict between Tom and his prospects; they were dissatisfied because he wasn't giving them what they wanted.)
- People do not always tell you when they are in conflict with you. (Tom had received no feedback from his prospects about his listening failure.)
- Many times our communication challenges impact us in both work and home. (Tom's listening affected both his business and his relationship with his wife.)
- Listening with the wrong style can cause conflict.

I heard a saying once that went, "No one cares how much you know until they know how much you care." I really believe that this is true. However, caring can take many different forms. Some of Tom's clients felt cared for by his style of listening and questioning. Others did not. Tom needed to consider each of the five forms of listening to relate to his potential clients.

Appreciative listening

Individuals in the appreciative listening mode are listening in order to enjoy the listening experience. Their focus is to relax while they are listening.

Appreciative listeners are motivated by enjoyment. Appreciative listening is very appropriate at times. If someone tells you a joke or a good story, it would be appropriate to be using appreciative listening. Other events such as going to a concert, a comedy club, or any pleasurable activity would likely match well with an appreciative listening style. When I do seminars on listening, I symbolize appreciative listening by giving a participant a television remote control. This demonstrates how the appreciative listener may "switch the channel" if they loose interest in what you are saying. Have you ever been talking to someone about a problem and you can see in his or her eyes that the lights are on, but nobody is home? They are off thinking about something that is more interesting to them than what you are saying. They are in the appreciative listening mode and obviously they are appreciating something besides your problem situation.

Empathic listening

Individuals in the empathic listening mode are listening in order to support the person speaking. Their focus is to show concern for the person talking. Empathic listeners are motivated by their desire to impact the person talking by providing them an opportunity to express their feelings. Again, there is no right or wrong to empathic listening, but rather there are situations that naturally call for this type of listening and others that call for different styles. Empathic listening is appropriate when you are counseling a friend, letting someone blow off steam, or bonding with someone with whom you want a good relationship. In my listening seminars I try to pick a burly looking guy and I give him this absolutely atrocious-looking big red heart pillow that says "I love you" on it. I jokingly use this to demonstrate the amount of care that the empathic listener gives by his head nods and caring questions. If someone is looking for empathic listening, then nodding and showing care is great. If they are not, then this style can be annoying to them.

Comprehensive listening

Individuals in the comprehensive listening mode are listening in order to organize the information being given by the speaker. Their focus is to make sense out of the information. They are motivated by the chance to apply what they are hearing to their own personal experience. They enjoy picking out the main idea and supporting ideas to help create an organized message. Comprehensive listening has its uses and is most appropriate for situations like taking direction from someone, helping a peer make sense of scattered thoughts, or trying to determine an action to take. In my listening seminars I symbolize the comprehensive listening style by giving someone a labeling gun. People use labeling guns to organize things. Labels give them a structure, which often gives them comfort. You can tell by the questions of the comprehensive listeners that they are labeling and organizing your statements.

Discerning listening

Individuals in the discerning listening mode are listening in order to gather information. Their focus is to get the complete picture and information. They are motivated by the desire to find the main message, sort out the details, and to pinpoint what is important about what the speaker is saying. Discerning listening is most appropriate in learning situations where your goal is to gather as much information as possible. In my seminars I take out a dusty old tan overcoat and put it on one of the participants. I have them bend over slightly and look up and say, "Oh, just one more question." Many people in the audience immediately recognize the reference to the television detective Columbo. Columbo would spend the entire show not looking like he knew what he was doing. He just kept asking questions over and over. And there was always one more question. He would do this until he had gathered all of the information necessary to put the puzzle together, and then he would nail the bad guy. Discerning listeners usually have lots of questions when you are speaking with them.

Evaluative listening

Individuals in the evaluative listening mode are listening in order to move to action and fix the situation. Their focus is on making a decision from the available information. They are motivated to relate information to their personal beliefs and question motives behind the message. They do this in order to accept or reject the message and move to action or fix the problem. Evaluative listening is appropriate when you need to make a decision, vote on something, or draw conclusions to move toward fixing something. In my seminars I give the participant representing the evaluative listener a wrench to represent their style of just getting enough information so they can make a decision and move on. To demonstrate how this leads to conflict, I have the person with the wrench square off against the person with the heart. This gives a visual representation to the audience of how listening in a style different than what the person is looking for can lead to problems.

Without fail, when I do my listening seminar someone asks me how you can tell what style someone is looking for. I often reflect the challenge back to the audience and they start building complicated systems for assessing the desired listening style. Eventually one brave soul will quietly chime in, "Uh, couldn't you just ask them what they need from you?" At this point the lights usually go on for the audience. Sometimes we make communication too difficult. If you want to know what someone needs from you, just ask. Let them tell you if they just want you to enjoy a story, or if they need your support, or if they want help to organize their thoughts, or if they just want you to ask good questions. Every now and then you may actually get someone who wants you to help him make a decision or fix a problem. When you listen to people in the way they need to be heard, you can decrease the risk for negative conflict. When you listen to people in a style different than what they want, you will miss their main message and likely frustrate them. This, of course, increases the chances for misunderstandings and upset feelings. In our story, Tom was having conflict that he didn't even realizing he was having. This was impacting his business and his marriage. Tom was not a bad or uncaring man, he just had to learn a lesson about listening to others in the way they want to be heard.

Exercises
Self-reflection exercise: What is your style of listening?
Answer the following questions:

Given the descriptions above, which of the five listening styles do you use most often at work?_____

How well does your main listening style fit the style that is most appropriate for your work situation? What changes (if any) do you need to make in this style?

Which of the five styles do you use most frequently at home (or with friends if you live alone)?_____

How well does this match up with what the people at home (or friends) want from you? What changes (if any) do you need to make in this style?

Knowledge challenge exercise: How does listening style impact people at work?

Read the following story and answer the questions:

Taylor was a new manager who had just been assigned her first employee to manage. Like most beginning managers, Taylor was both excited and somewhat intimidated at the idea of actually managing someone. The employee that she was to manage, Sue, seemed eager to be coached by her, and it looked as though they were off to a good start. However, within a couple of months, Sue was repeatedly bringing up difficulties that she was having with a coworker. Being unsure of the best way to deal with the situation, Taylor focused on showing understanding and care each time Sue brought up the different situations with her coworker.

It soon became evident that the way Taylor was dealing with the situation was not helping. Sue continued to bring up this "annoying coworker" week after week. Taylor started asking more questions about what the coworker was doing that was irritating Sue so much. Their sessions seemed to turn into laundry lists of this other person's behavior. After time, Taylor started to get irritated herself, but not at the coworker. Rather, she was getting sick and tired of Sue's whining and complaining. Eventually she began to dread her coaching sessions with Sue and even found herself postponing and rescheduling their time together.

Imagine that Taylor brings the situation to you. As Taylor's manager, how would you answer the following questions:
What are the main issues in this situation?

What would you do in order to help Taylor in this situation?

What does Taylor need to do?

These questions are mainly to help you think through the issues. If you would like to see our answers to them you can find them listed in the appendix in the back of this book.

Next steps and additional resources

Experiment with the listening styles. Notice what types of questions you ask and what types of responses you give depending on your choice of style. Notice what listening style others are using with you. Pay attention to how you feel when someone is using the wrong style (one different than what you are looking for). If you are in a close relationship, talk to him or her about the listening styles. Ask for feedback on which style is most helpful to the other person. Make a commitment to improve your listening so that unnecessary conflict can be avoided.

If you would like to gain insight into your own listening style, you can order a self-contained profile to assess yourself from Advantage Coaching & Training. Also, you can find a video recording of a live demonstration of the listening styles on "Critical Coaching Skills Video #2: Dealing with Difficult People." Information for ordering each of these can be found in the back of the book.

> *"Most people do not listen with the intent to understand;*
> *they listen with the intent to reply."*
>
> —Stephen R. Covey,
> *The Seven Habits of Highly Effective People*

> *"My dear brothers, take note of this: Everyone should be*
> *quick to listen, slow to speak, and slow to become angry,*
> *for man's anger does not bring about the righteous*
> *life that God desires."*
>
> —James 1:19

Chapter 14:

Four Communication Patterns to Use if You Want to Keep Fighting

Sometimes conflict comes not from what we say, but rather how we say it. There are several patterns of communication that have potential for creating conflict. These patterns are barriers to good communication, and as long as we interact with each other in this way, we limit our chances for truly resolving conflict. In this chapter we will review four communication patterns that will almost guarantee conflict. We will then look at a fifth way to communicate that can diffuse conflict even in difficult situations.

Real life

For our real life example, I want to share a story from a previous book I've written called *The Coach's Handbook: Exercises for Resolving Conflict in the Workplace.* I often use this story in seminars to demonstrate just how negative communication patterns can affect a work team.

Hank had a problem with his colleague, Dan. He would lose sleep for days when he knew that he would be assigned to a project with Dan. Dan was the ultimate critic; nothing was ever good enough for him, especially the little insights that Hank was able to generate during their team meetings. These meetings usually started with Dan complaining about having too many projects on his plate and ended with Dan subtly discounting any suggestions offered by Hank or other team members. Most of Hank's coworkers dealt with Dan by ignoring him. Hank tried for months to work with Dan, but was continually frustrated by his inability to satisfy him and was becoming very angry inside. He tried every approach he could think of and each one failed miserably.

Hank was also frustrated with his supervisor (who was very aware of Dan's negative attitudes and behavior). Hank once asked him why he never stood up to Dan. His supervisor mumbled a statement about Dan's ability to perform in the field and told Hank that he needed to be a little "thicker-skinned" about the whole thing.

At one of their meetings, Dan started blaming Hank for a delay in the project that clearly was not Hank's fault. This was the last straw for Hank. He thought, "Will no one stand up to this jerk?" Then he let him have it! Hank blasted Dan with months of frustration, focusing on Dan's critical nature and constant "whininess." Hank ended his tirade by slamming his fist down on the desk and walking out of the room.

Throughout the next week, Dan gave Hank the cold shoulder. Several of Hank's coworkers asked him to go talk to Dan and see if he could smooth things over. Dan was hard enough to work with when he wasn't offended, let alone when he was carrying a chip on his shoulder. After much resistance, Hank finally gave in. The next day he apologized to Dan in order to please the rest of the team. He felt defeated and abandoned by team, and felt a loss of self-respect from both his outbreaks of anger and his pacifying.

How it applies

Who was wrong in the above example? Was it Hank? Dan? The supervisor? The team? If you answered "everybody," then you are correct. Each coped with conflict in a different, but equally unhealthy manner. The following four unhealthy communication styles are adapted from the classic work of a therapist named Virginia Satir. Her work with family communication transfers well to all forms of communication both at work and home. The four communication styles that I see most often in my work are:

- Criticism
- Rationalization
- Pacification
- Withdrawal

Criticism

Critics act as though they think they are superior to other people. They are judgmental, blunt, and demeaning, and they enjoy showing their power and importance at the expense of others. They are experts at giving you messages such as, *"You* failed me," "I am disappointed in y*ou,"* *"You* will never get it," or, "Don't *you* have a brain in your body?" The critic enjoys it when others cower to their authority. Sometimes people act as though they are superior because they actually think they are better than others. Sometimes they act superior because their self-esteem is extremely low and they are trying to prove themselves. On other occasions, people shift to the critical mode as a defense because it feels safer than feeling hurt. Finally, at times people who are being critical are that way because they simply have let their frustration build up too much. They failed to address the issue when they could have dealt with it in a healthier way.

Pacification

The pacifying person does his or her best to calm down the other person in the conversation even at the sake of standing up for personal beliefs. Pacifying is often motivated by fear. Pacifiers try to appease the other person at the cost of their own dignity and honor. By pacifying, they believe they can avoid the other person's wrath. However, they perpetuate the underlying conflict issues because they never confront the issues. By taking a weaker position, they hope to control the criticism of the other person. They want to get rid of the conflict even at the sake of their own self-respect and genuineness. A lifetime of pacifying can lead to bitterness and/or depression. In addition, the goal of the pacifier is often not achieved by his strategy. Often they actually increase the anger of the other person for several reasons. For example, if the other person is being critical, then the pacifying may make him feel even more powerful. Therefore he may take the critical mode up a notch. Often, people lose respect for pacifiers, which of course makes the conflict even worse. The goal of the person pacifying (decreasing the conflict) fails, and the longer-term conflict is never resolved. The conflict becomes a recurring discussion in their relationship with the other person.

Rationalization

Being logical and rational in conflict is a good thing—up to a point. Being rational means that you understand your emotions and that you base what you feel on what is true. Rationalizers, on the other hand, are people who depend too much on intellect and logic in conflict situations. They see emotions as unnecessary and feel superior to people who show emotions in an argument. When someone approaches them with a conflict, they often accuse that person of being irrational, or they attempt to bypass an emotional discussion by immediately shifting to problem-solving. This can cause the other person to feel dismissed or demeaned. The rationalizer is often clueless to what he feels. He has a wall around his heart and lets few (if any) see what he really feels. He is like the tortoise who escapes to his shell during conflict. He simply hides his retreat by focusing on logic and cognition rather than emotion. He may look like he is facing the conflict with a cool confidence, but truthfully he is hiding behind his shell in fear.

Withdrawal

Withdrawing is simply the avoidance of dealing with conflict. You can withdraw emotionally by telling someone that nothing is wrong even when you are quite upset, or you can withdraw physically by actually leaving the room. Now, there is a time and place to say to another individual:

> *"I can feel myself getting too upset about this and I need a little time to calm down so I can handle this well. This discussion is important to me and I will call you tonight to try to work through it with you."*

This approach often demonstrates wisdom and not withdrawing. In withdrawing, you basically guarantee that the issue can never be addressed. It prohibits the entire possibility of conflict resolution. People who withdraw use silence, emotional coldness, and distance as weapons or instruments of protection. At times, they will withdraw in order to punish or manipulate the other person. People can withdraw in order to abandon someone until he will change his behavior. Other times, they withdraw because they feel frightened or helpless to change the situation. On these occasions, their withdrawal is based on despair rather than manipulation.

Communications style analysis

Using these descriptions, go back to our example with Hank and see if you can identify the style shown by the following people:

- Hank at first
- Hank's later reaction
- Other team members
- Dan
- The supervisor

After you have attempted this yourself, come back to the following sentences and read my interpretation of the interactions.

In my mind, each of the team members involved showed the following negative communication patterns:

- Hank's main style was pacifying to Dan's wishes. When enough frustration built up, he became very aggressive and critical himself. However, when the team pushed him to apologize, he quickly reverted to his pacifying position.
- The team members' main style was avoidance. They refused to deal with the issues with Dan and rather avoided conflict. They even pushed Hank to apologize in order for the issue to "disappear."
- Dan obviously had a critical style and stayed true to form throughout the example. Everyone seemed afraid of dealing with his behavior and thus reinforced it.
- The supervisor used rationalization. All that he could see was that Dan was a producer for the company. He was not aware of the emotional implications of Dan's behavior and how that would eventually hurt the company.

We each can fall into these styles during the times when we are communicating poorly. Even if you and your spouse, friends, or colleagues have great communication most of the time, you will occasionally take on one of these roles. However, if you grow to understand these tendencies and realize when you are falling into the patterns, you will be able to catch yourself and switch your behavior to a more effective style.

Eye-to-eye communication

As stated in the title of this chapter, these are communication patterns to use if you never want to resolve a conflict. However, I feel it is safe to assume that anyone picking up this book would be very interested in decreasing the number of conflicts in life, so we need to talk about a fifth style. The fifth pattern is the pattern to use if you want to increase your chances for healthy conflict resolution. I call it the eye-to-eye approach.

The eye-to-eye communication has the following characteristics:

- It is respectful
- It is genuine
- It is honest
- It is equal (no one is above or below the other person)
- It is vulnerable
- It is hard to do

How refreshing is it to have a disagreement with someone and yet feel his total respect during the entire conversation? It is quite a breath of fresh air. Equally refreshing is knowing that, while respectful, the person is also genuinely being himself and telling you the truth as he knows it. He does not feel superior or inferior to you. Rather, you are two equally valuable adults having an openly vulnerable discussion. However, this type of communication is hard to do. You may be eye-to-eye and the other person could withdraw or be disrespectful and attacking in return. This feels particularly hurtful when you have been so vulnerable. I believe that is why it is so difficult for people to stay in the eye-to-eye pattern. However, I have found that if you have the strength, courage, and tenacity to stay in the eye-to-eye pattern no matter what the other person does, then eventually most people will respond well to you and will become more respectful. They may try your patience in the amount of time it takes them to respond, but the rewards for your persistence can be great. Unfortunately, many unnecessary conflicts are caused by the inability for either person to keep eye-to-eye conversation going.

Exercises
Self-reflection exercise: Name your pattern
Using the previous descriptions of the styles as your guide, answer the following questions:

Choose either your work or home life and think about those occasions (even if rare) when you are not communicating well. Put a percentage to indicate how often you fall into each of the patterns. Since we are only looking at times that you communicate poorly, your total should add up to 100 percent.

Critical	_____
Pacifying	_____
Rationalizing	_____
Avoiding	_____
Total:	_____

Examine the role you take most often. What motivates you to take that role? How does it serve you? How does it hurt you?

Brainstorm about a time in your life when you handled a conflict well. Journal below about how much you used an eye-to-eye pattern in that communication. How did it help? If you did not use the eye-to-eye method, write about how it could have gone even better using this pattern.

Next steps and additional resources

Again, it is very helpful to learn these patterns by analyzing the behavior of others. Record one of your favorite shows from the television. The show can be either a comedy or a drama, but has to involve a conflict between characters. Watch their conflict several times and see if you can map out their communication patterns. Note if they shift from one pattern to another in response to what the other person does. Examine how this reflects on your own life.

For further information on the work of Virginia Satir, try *People Making.*

"An appeaser is one who feeds a crocodile,
hoping it will eat him last."

—Winston Churchhill

"We must combine the toughness of the serpent
and the softness of the dove,
a tough mind and a tender heart."

—Martin Luther King Jr.

"Love and compassion are necessities, not luxuries.
Without them humanity cannot survive."

—Dalai Lama

Chapter 15

Don't Assume the Position

Conflict escalates when people become rigid about a single way to reach the result that they want. When two individuals each pick a single opposing solution to a problem, positive resolution is unlikely. This rigidity causes endless arguments with each person arguing his position. Fortunately, we are intelligent creatures who, if we take the time, can figure out multiple solutions to any problem. Many times these solutions will come when we understand what is *really* driving our perspective. When we know our core want then we can problem-solve multiple ways to meet this need. In this chapter we will look at positions and wants (or interests) and how they impact the conflict coward.

Real life

➜ Jim's wife walked in the room on a warm Saturday afternoon. Jim looked up from the television where he was watching his usual sports event. As they caught eyes, Jim's wife said, "I'm sick and tired of always coming second in your life. I want a divorce."

➜ Dawn's boss called her into his office and curtly said to her, "If you don't land a new account by the end of the month I am going to have to let you go." Dawn left the office in silence fearing for her job.

➜ Dale's client was unhappy with the result of Dale's work. The client left Dale a voicemail saying, "This is not the type of work I expect from someone of your quality. Maybe we need to find a different person to outsource this project to." At that moment Dale wrote off the client in his mind and never expected to get any work from him again.

→ Sally was a highly valued employee working in a small business. The business owner valued her contribution and compensated her accordingly. Sally found great fulfillment in her career, but also valued contributing to her children's lives by being highly available for them. As it became more and more difficult to balance her work and family, she told her boss that she needed to quit the job. Her boss begged her to stay, but Sally couldn't stand the pressure of working full-time and caring for her family.

How it applies

In *Getting to Yes: Negotiating Agreement Without Giving In*, authors Roger Fisher, William Ury, and Bruce Patton describe the difference between a position and an interest. Simply put, a position is a way to get what you want. An interest is what you really want. In the examples above, everyone is focused on positions rather than interests. In other words, they are only considering one way to get what they want; they are only considering one position. Let's take each of the examples to examine this process. Please note that I will be providing possible interests for each situation, but we do not really know the true interests. In fact, most of the potential interests that I will be sharing could be positions. Only by talking about the issue with the other person and asking powerful questions can we really distinguish positions from interests. However, let's look at some possible interests beneath each of the examples.

→ *"I'm sick and tired of always coming second in your life. I want a divorce."*
   Jim's wife says she wants a divorce. However, is that truly what she wants? What are some other possible wants? It is quite possible that what she really wants is:

- To feel loved
- To be attended to more than sports
- To feel important
- To feel respected

These wants are all possible interests. The statement of wanting a divorce is a position. A divorce is one way to get out of the relationship and get into one that is more loving and respectful. However, there are other ways to get those same results. Perhaps if Jim turned off the television more often and spent more time with her, she would be satisfied and not want a divorce. If Jim misses this point and only focuses on the divorce statement, they will both miss the core issue driving the discussion and likely fail to resolve the real issue.

➜ *"If you don't land a new account by the end of the month I am going to have to let you go."*

Dawn's boss made a threat that caught Dawn's attention. His position is that she needs to land a new account or she will lose her job. What are some possible interests beneath that position? Dawn's boss may:

- Be interested in the company making more money
- Be worried that his boss will blame him if his department doesn't raise more new business
- Think that Dawn isn't working hard enough and wants to motivate her

At face value, Dawn will lose her job if she doesn't bring in new business, but perhaps there are other ways to deal with the boss's interests. Perhaps a current client could be tapped into to increase revenue. Perhaps a work plan could be developed that would show her boss that she is truly trying. Perhaps Dawn could approach her boss with training needs that could help him feel confident that new business will come in the future. Again, there are many ways to negotiate and resolve the issue. This will only work if Dawn and her boss can figure out and focus on the true interests rather than the position.

➜ *"This is not the type of work that I expect from someone of your quality. Maybe we need to find a different person to outsource this project to."*

Dale's client was obviously displeased with Dale's work, but what is his true interest? Does he really want to find a different person to do the job? We get a hint of this by his statement of Dale's work usually being of high quality. This tells us that the client was not assuming that this job fairly represented Dale's abilities. Therefore, what are some possible interests? Dale's client may:

- Want the job to be fixed to a higher level of quality
- Want Dale to give him a refund or discount
- Want Dale to know that he is upset and to apologize
- Want to make certain that Dale is not taking advantage of him

If Dale and his client only consider the one position of outsourcing the job to a different person then both are going to be disappointed. However, if Dale can wisely discuss the issue with his client and figure out what he really wants, then they can creatively find ways to meet the interests and still keep a good relationship.

➔ *Sally couldn't stand the pressure.*

Sally found fulfillment in both career and family, but found the two of them in conflict. Did Sally really want to quit her job, or was that the only position that she was considering? Her interest was not to quit her job. She liked her job, she just did not like feeling as though she was not doing her best both as an employee and a mother. Her true interests could have been:

- A balance between work and home
- To get rid of the guilt of not doing her best at either work or home
- To have more flexibility in her life

There are many solutions to this challenge. What if Sally and her boss could get to the real interests and become very creative. Maybe Sally could cut back her hours and/or job-share with another individual. Or she could get a more flexible schedule, including the ability to do some work from home. The possible solutions are many. However, as long as the focus is on the position of quitting work, then both Sally and her boss's creative energies are wasted.

Position vs. interest

So how do you figure out what is a position and what is an interest? One simple method is to use the following series of statements and questions.

Step 1: Say, "I really want to understand what it is that you want. I hear you saying that you want _____. Is that correct?"

Step 2: Let them clarify what they want.

Step 3: Ask, "I'm wondering if we can be creative about figuring this out. Would you mind telling me what is driving your want for _____? In other words, why do you want it?" Make sure your voice is nonjudgmental.

Step 4: Listen (repeat this step after each question. REALLY listen).

Step 5: Ask, "Is there something driving that want? What will having what you want do for you?"

Step 6: Ask, "And what would having that do for you?"

Step 7: Keep repeating this line of questioning until it seems like you have gotten down to the core interest.

Step 8: Reflect back to the other person your perception of the core interest.

Step 9: Creatively problem-solve how to get this interest met.

I will demonstrate this process in a story about a couple. Notice how Frank uses this technique with his wife Terri in the example below. This discussion now moves from a potential conflict to joint problem-solving where each individual cares deeply about what the other person wants, and is trying to honor that want. Instead of fighting over differing wants they can now work together as a team to get what they both want.

> TERRI: I don't want to go to your company Christmas party this year.

> FRANK: I really want to understand what it is that you want. I hear you saying that you want to skip the party this year. Is that correct?

TERRI: That's right. I just don't want to go.

FRANK: Well, I would prefer it if we could talk this over. I'm wondering if we can be creative about figuring this out. Would you mind telling me what is driving your want for not going? In other words, why do you want to skip it?

TERRI: I have a lot on my plate right now and could use the time.

FRANK: Is there something driving your desire to get some time? What will having more time do for you?

TERRI: Well, for one thing, I can get all of the kids' presents wrapped and make sure that we have done all of our shopping.

FRANK: And what would getting those two things done do for you?

TERRI: It would reassure me that everything that needs to be done can get done.

FRANK: And what would having that reassurance do for you?

TERRI: I think that it would help me be more relaxed during the holidays, unlike previous years.

FRANK: And what would being more relaxed do for you?

TERRI: That's about it. It would just be more relaxing and enjoyable.

FRANK: OK, so if I understand you correctly, what you really want is to be more relaxed during this holiday season and skipping my office party is one way to do this. Is that correct?

TERRI: *Yes, that's it. I just don't want to be crazed this year.*

Frank: Well, I wonder if we can be creative so that we can both get what we want. I want you with me at the party and you want to get some things done so you can relax. Can we talk about what I can do that would help you be relaxed enough that you would feel OK about coming to the party? What are some tasks I can help with?

Many useless and destructive conflicts occur when people argue positions and fail to see the interests beneath the apparent differences.

Exercises
Self-reflection exercise: What were the interests?

Reflect on a past conflict you had where what the other person wanted seemed to conflict with what you said you wanted. Use the format below to examine the positions and interests.

Briefly describe the event:

What was the other person's stated position?

What was your position?

To the best of your ability, answer why they wanted what they said they wanted. (Try to give them the benefit of the doubt rather than assuming negative motivations.)

What would having this do for them? What might the core interest be?

Why did you want what you said you wanted?

What would having this do for you? What is your core interest?

Assuming that you are correct in your analysis of the interests, name three ways that the two of you could have creatively problem-solved so that both of you could have gotten what you really wanted.

If you are unable to do this for the conflict that you chose, then repeat the steps using a different conflict. If none of the conflicts that you choose are solvable, then you are likely not being creative enough.

Action exercise: Test your theory
Use your judgement to determine if it is wise (and/or possible) to approach the person listed in the exercise above. Share with them your work in this book and your desire to help them get what they want. Tell them that you want to check with them to see if you are assuming correctly when you tried to figure out what they wanted. Share your creative problem-solving with them and see how they respond.

Next steps and additional resources
Commit to yourself that you will use the steps presented in this chapter to help determine someone's interests rather than positions. Ask a friend with whom you are not in conflict to walk through the process with you. Have them tell you something they want and see if you can help them determine why they want what they think they want. In other words, help them determine their interests. Make sure you practice this *before* trying it in any conflictual situations.

For additional insights into positions and interests, try *Getting to Yes: Negotiating Agreement Without Giving In* by Roger Fisher, William Ury, and Bruce Patton.

"It is a luxury to be understood."

—Ralph Waldo Emerson

Chapter 16:

The Role of Selfishness

Have you heard the joke about the self-centered man? He is at a party talking to another guest. In the conversation he goes on and on for what must have been an hour about himself, his accomplishments, his likes and dislikes, and his various views of the world. Finally after droning on a few moments more, he takes a breath. The person with whom he is talking feels relief that the conversation is about to switch to another topic. Just then the self-centered man looks at the person he is talking to and says, "But enough about me, what do you think of me?" This joke captures the essence of this chapter. Few things play out more in conflict than selfishness. In this chapter we will examine several different forms of selfishness and how each form can create harmful conflict.

Real life

As was often the case, the reason that Gary called me for coaching was not the real reason at all. Gary had been the top sales leader in his company for the past three years. Being the best meant long hours and lots of travel, but Gary had a dream. He wanted to retire by the time he was fifty. He called me and said that he wanted career coaching. He then asked if his wife could come in to his first session. This was an unusual request, but I am flexible about these things and always trust that there is a good reason for a request. His stated goal of career coaching was not entirely false, but as we talked in my office, it was obvious to me that he knew exactly what he wanted out of his career. His wife, Jean, had been quiet for most of the session, so I attempted to get her to participate a little bit. "So, Jean, what do you think about all of this?" I asked (OK, it is not a brilliant question, but sometimes the simple ones do the job). Jean responded, "I know that Gary wants to retire early, but I have been thinking lately that I'd like us to start trying to have a baby." Gary quickly jumped in the conversation and it went something like this:

GARY: Jean, you know I work hard and I just want to be able to stop this mad pace before I'm too old to enjoy my life. When we got married I assumed that we were not going to have children.

JEAN: I was busy with my own career when we got married, how could I have known how I would feel about having children? Every time I see my sister with her kids I just feel incredibly sad. There is more to life than money, and I don't care if we need to cut down. You work too hard anyway. I'm worried about your health and I just want you around more.

GARY: Well, that is just fine. Obviously, you are going to pressure me into doing things your way. I'm around plenty and kids were never part of the deal.

JEAN: This isn't about a deal, this is about our lives. I just won't be fulfilled if I don't have children. I have never denied you anything. How can you deny me this?

GARY: What do you mean you have never denied me anything? Are you joking? And you are certainly willing to deny me my early retirement, aren't you? All you care about is what you want!

JEAN: You just don't understand how a woman feels about these things.

> GARY: (turning to me) OK, Doc, this is where we get stuck. Now do some coaching magic and help us work through this.

> DOC TIM: Yikes!

Yes, "Yikes," was my initial internal response, but given that "yikes" would not give them much confidence in my ability to help them through this, I tried for a different approach. "OK, let me try something. It sounds like this is a conversation that you have had several times and not just today in my office. So Gary, without criticism or sarcasm, can you look at Jean and reflect back to her what she really wants and why she wants it." It took several false starts before Gary could do this without adding a little critical zinger into his reflection. After he got it right, I asked Jean to do the same thing by reflecting back to Gary, without criticism, what he really wanted and why he wanted it. She was able to do it on the first try, but did it with a spirit of someone who was resigned and helpless. I asked her to do it again with the spirit of someone who really cared about what Gary wanted. Eventually, she was able to do this (especially when I was able to convince her that showing that she understood what Gary wanted did not mean that she agreed with it).

"So, who is wrong in what they want?" I challenged them. "Well, no one is really wrong" was the predicted response that they gave so I went on, "That's interesting because to an outside observer it looks like you are treating each other like one of you is wrong." I then spent the session exploring this communication observation with them. By the end of the session, Gary and Jean were able to see that they were each approaching the issue from a selfish perspective. They made a commitment to work through the issue, but their commitment did not resolve the issue right away. It took weeks of examining the options, problem-solving, and lots of creativity for them to come up with a solution that was right for them. The solution is irrelevant. The process is crucial. If they had continued on their original course, then you could predict one of three outcomes:

> Gary would give in and be resentful.
> Jean would give in and be resentful
> The marriage would end.

By facing their selfishness and truly working to care about what the other person wanted, they strengthened their marriage rather than destroyed it.

How it applies

Some people just see the world one way—their way. Self-centeredness thrives in the culture of the United States. Think of all of the songs that are about justified selfishness:

> Frank Sinatra sings, "I did it my way."
>
> Janet Jackson sings, "I've gotta be the one in control."
>
> Billy Joel belts out, "I don't care what you say anymore, this is my life."
>
> N*Sync charms us with, "It's gonna be me."

In our example above, who was selfish? Of course, the answer is both of them. Your perspective on this could be tainted by what you value. If you value career over family, you likely see Jean as the selfish one. If you value family over career, Gary is the selfish brat! In truth, while having different styles of expressing themselves, they both were focused on what they wanted and not what the other person wanted.

We love to focus on ourselves don't we? Oh, we don't like to appear selfish, but deep down we all have selfish tendencies. Some of us are obviously selfish and others of us are much more subtle in our selfishness. But before we discuss blatant and subtle selfishness I want to differentiate between self-care and selfishness.

Self-care is essential for living a fulfilling life, and there is nothing wrong with it. In fact, healthy self-care is shown by the analogy commonly used by coaches of a plane incident when the cabin loses pressure. The flight attendants remind us every time we fly that if we are traveling with small children then we should put the oxygen mask on ourselves first and *then* on the children. If we do not take care of ourselves in this way then we cannot take care of others effectively. It is only when we practice self-care at the expense of others that we really need to examine whether it has fallen into the realm of selfishness. The selfish individual does not care how his or her actions impact someone else. With extreme selfishness, the needs of others are irrelevant. A person who shows healthy self-care balances her needs with the needs of others involved and does not show a pattern of consistently picking her needs over the needs of others. While there is no right equation to determine when you cross the line from self-care to selfishness, the most important factor is the level of care you have for what the other person wants. When your care for their wants is close to your care for your own wants, you are stepping out of a selfish perspective.

Some selfishness is so blatant that you can't miss it: someone cuts in front of you in the line at an amusement park. Someone steals from another person. Someone sabotages your work project in order to get ahead of you in the game. These are pretty obvious. The blatantly selfish person makes no qualms about what he wants. He declares it in word or action and seems to show no shame. Rather, he feels entitled to get what he wants. BSP's (blatantly selfish persons) are easy to spot, yet not easy to deal with. If they do not see anything wrong with their behavior, then there will be no motivation to change.

Subtly selfish persons (SSP's) are much less obvious in their selfishness. In our previous example, Jean talked about caring for Gary's health and just wanting to be with him. On the surface, this appears to be very noble. However, one has to question what was really fueling those statements. Was she really focused on him, or were those statements merely tools to help her get what she wanted without looking selfish? People often use emotional pain as a way to get what they want without appearing selfish. SSP's learn to talk about their fear and hurt feelings to help manipulate the other people involved. Now I am not demeaning emotional pain by any means. However, our highly therapized society has sometimes given too much ground to emotional pain. We see the person as a victim rather than a powerful person who is able (and responsible) to work though the pain. SSP's expect others to work around their pain. In my mind, Jean's focus on the deprivation that she would feel if she didn't have children is no more and no less selfish than Gary's desire to retire early. I admit that the two issues "feel" different emotionally, and if you had asked me years ago who was more selfish, I would have picked out Gary in a second. However, I've since learned that selfishness has many hidden forms and faces. Do not misunderstand me, I am not saying that Jean's feelings are wrong or irrelevant. They are extremely important! However, her feelings are not more "right" than Gary's desires. They both have merit. They both have value. And neither one should *dictate* what the answer to the conflict should be.

Subtle selfishness can take many forms:

- The spouse who refuses to drive again after being in a car accident and thus hampers the activities of their husband or wife
- The manager who tends to always get his name connected to a project where you did all of the work
- The coworker who apologetically comes late to your lunch appointment because he wanted to finish a project that he was working on before he came

We can argue over the degree of selfishness shown in each of these, but to do so misses the point. The point is that selfishness can hide itself well, but it continues to be equally destructive when we are unwilling to name it.

I use to believe that I was an extremely unselfish individual and I would have continued believing that if not for two things. First was a book by Larry Crabb called *Men and Women: Enjoying the Difference*. The book does an excellent job of shedding light on all forms of selfishness. The second thing that helped reveal my subtle selfishness was a commitment that my wife and I made years ago to start something called a marriage accountability group. Through our church, we connected with several other couples for what started out as a Bible study group. However, we were not happy with the level of intimacy that the usual study group had and decided to do something different. Most people are very secretive about their marriage issues unless they are simply complaining to someone who they know will support them. We decided that it would unique to have a group dedicated to growing our marriages.

We decided to read the Crabb book as a group, which was helpful. However, the most helpful thing we did was make a commitment to come to the group each week and take turns admitting where we were selfish in our marriages that week. Talk about pressure! And I was pretty sure that if I did not confess how I was selfish during the week, my wife would be kind enough to chime in with some examples. This action was life-changing and was the beginning of the journey where I found out just how foul my subtle selfishness can be. I still can be very selfish and self-focused, and it is a continual struggle to catch this and change it. However, I can go into situations understanding myself well and have a much better chance of catching my selfishness. The accountability of the group helps greatly.

Allow me to make one last point about selfishness. Some people have spent their lives giving to others and denying what they want. I am not an advocate of codependency. In fact, I think it is impossible to truly give to another person out of a pure heart unless you have the ability to give yourself permission to say no. Think about it. If I automatically give you your way, then am I really giving unselfishly or have I just been programmed to do so? However, if you know beyond a shadow of a doubt that I fully have the ability to say "no" to you concerning something that you want, and yet I still say "yes," then you know I have truly decided to be unselfish in the situation. If I can't deny you what you want, then I really don't have the ability to show selflessness in giving it to you.

Selfishness causes conflict. Balancing self-care and a deep care for others creates a spirit of compromise and a desire to help everyone feel fulfilled in what they truly desire.

Exercises
Self-reflection exercise: Selfishness

Reflect upon a reoccurring conflict you continue to have with the same person and answer the following questions:

How is the other person showing selfishness in the situation? Is it blatant or subtle?

How are you showing selfishness in the situation? Is it blatant or subtle?

If you were to completely see their side of it, what do they really want or need? (Do not allow yourself to be critical or sarcastic in this analysis.)

Brainstorm about a possible solution that would allow both of you to get some of what you really want.

Approach the other person this week and tell him that you are trying to understand what he is feeling and wanting in the conflict. You do not need to make any commitments to do anything for him, but just reflect back to him what you think he feels and wants. Ask him to clarify anything that you don't seem to understand. After you get his agreement that you understand him completely, ask him if he is willing to walk through the same exercise trying to connect with what you want. If it seems appropriate, share some of your ideas from question #4 above and ask for other ideas from him. After this discussion, record your observations.

What is your next step in resolving this conflict?

Next steps and additional resources

Ask someone who will be completely honest with you to give you feedback on your balance between self-care and the care of others. Be open to how selfishness and selflessness play a role in your life. The next time someone asks you to do something for them, make sure that you are able to say "no" before you consider saying "yes." Analyze any confrontations you have this week. Explore the role of selfishness in the disagreement. Try to look at the situation from all angles so that you can pick up both forms of selfishness: blatant and subtle.

For more insight on the role of selfishness, try *Men and Women: Enjoying the Difference* by Larry Crabb. For more on a marriage accountability group, try *Authentic Marriages* by our former group members Jeff and Lora Helton.

> *"There are two kinds of egotists:*
> *Those who admit it, and the rest of us."*
> —Laurence J. Peter

Chapter 17:

If Common Sense Is So Common, Then Why Don't They Have It?

I chuckle inside when someone says, "Just use common sense." I usually want to ask him if I should use his or mine. You see, we all have unique ways of perceiving the world. All of us walk around with thoughts in our head that are not fully based on reality. Our thoughts are based on our *perception* of reality. When thoughts are not based on reality and they are harmful, they are considered irrational thoughts. We all have them and we all are impacted by other people who also have them. Irrational thoughts are a great source of unnecessary and harmful conflict. In this chapter we will learn that the better control we have over them, the greater control we have when we enter a conflict situation.

Real life

Kyle was a small business owner who was referred to me for coaching by a close friend of his. The friend had attended a training session that I had done on selling to different behavioral styles and thought that her friend could benefit from some techniques for building his business. After a few sessions, Kyle started confiding in me that he wanted to work on more than his marketing plan. In reality he was having multiple challenges with his business.

> *KYLE:*
> - I have an assistant who demeans me in front of customers, but I'm afraid to say anything to her.
> - I start getting nervous every time I start making more money in my business.

- I'm afraid that someone will discover someday that I don't know what I'm doing.
- Some of my customers take advantage of me because they know I won't fight them.

It was obvious from Kyle's revelation that we had work to do before we started building his marketing plan.

Using the technique of TruthTalk (a technique which will be outlined for you in chapter 18), we were able to discover that Kyle had some core beliefs that were interfering with him taking his business to the next level. These core beliefs were:

KYLE:
- It is safer to be unsuccessful than to be successful.
- I don't deserve to be treated with respect.

Kyle grew to understand that these core beliefs had been with him for most of his life. Unfortunately, thoughts that have consciously or subconsciously plagued you for decades cannot usually be shifted with one insight. Therefore, Kyle and I worked up an entire strategy for attacking these self-lies. One of Kyle's first responses to TruthTalk was that he hated positive thinking approaches. He mockingly said, "I am the best business owner in the world and my life is great!" in his best sarcastic tone. I quickly agreed with him in his dislike of overly positive self-talk techniques. In my mind, some of these strategies trade irrational negative lies with irrational positive lies. Both Kyle and I agreed that whatever he was saying to himself should be based on truth, not pumped-up optimism. As you will learn in chapter 18, the TruthTalk system does not depend on irrational lies to make someone feel better. Rather, the entire strategy is based on learning how to say powerful *truths* to yourself.

Kyle and I worked on building new thoughts that he could fall back to when the old negative thoughts returned. These new beliefs were:

- It is safer to be in control of my success than to be controlled by past lies. I will keep my focus on doing what is right and let my successes flow from there. Living with integrity is more important than living with false safety.

- My true belief is that everyone deserves to be treated with respect. I refuse to have different rules for myself. I will only expect the same level of respect that I am willing to give.

I encouraged Kyle to put the new true beliefs in his daytimer where he could look at them every day. He went one step further and posted them on his bathroom mirror so that he would be reminded of them constantly. Whenever he started having doubts, he would pull them out again. It was a daily and then weekly battle to keep his mind on the truth. Eventually, his persistence paid off. The old thoughts plagued him less and less as time went on. His new thoughts became more automatic. He no longer needed to view his index cards every day or even every week.

Kyle's behaviors started matching his new thoughts. He was showing great follow-through with the marketing plan that we finally developed. His finances were increasing and he wasn't doing anything to sabotage the progress. His confidence grew, and he started showing more self-respect. He gracefully stood up to his assistant who would demean him in front of customers. To his surprise, she stopped putting him down when he showed her that he would not allow the behavior to continue. Even customers decreased their unreasonable demands as they saw that he did not invite them to take advantage of him anymore (more on this inviting principle later).

As of this writing, Kyle is a very satisfied and prosperous individual. He has more than doubled his business, he is confident of his abilities and vision, and he has several people working for him who respect him completely. Kyle is in control of his perceptions. His irrational thoughts no longer control him unless he chooses to let them.

How it applies

As you can tell from the above example, Kyle's irrational thoughts not only impacted his ability to handle conflict, but also impacted his ability to be as successful as he could potentially be. Kyle is not alone in his struggle with irrational thinking. We all can have this struggle, and irrational thinking can influence conflict in several ways. It plays out in conflict in the following ways:

- Irrational thoughts can influence our behavior so that we subconsciously invite others to take advantage of us.
- Irrational thoughts can make us panic at the first sign of conflict and thus cause us to avoid it.
- Irrational thoughts can cause conflict by getting people upset when there is nothing to be upset about.
- Even if we should be a little upset, irrational thoughts can worsen conflict by exaggerating our level of emotion.

In the story presented about Kyle, irrational thinking mainly operated in the first category. By Kyle's sense of low self-worth and his undeserving attitude, he was subconsciously inviting people to demean him or treat him with less respect. Do you believe that? Do you believe that you can actually invite someone to mistreat you without even realizing it? I have no doubt this is true. I have seen this pattern in hundreds of individuals I have coached and I have seen it in myself.

My parents divorced for the second time when I was in ninth grade. I chose to move with my mother, and that meant starting anew at yet another school (we moved frequently as I was growing up). During the first week of school, I was devastated. My family life was in shambles, my mother was hurting terribly, and I was thrust into a new world with people I didn't know. My self-esteem was never that high to begin with, and the situation only made it worse. That first week in school I walked around with my head down, trapped in my own sadness. It didn't take long before the sharks smelled the blood in the water. I was walking down the busy hall after lunch when three "jocks" grabbed me, picked me up, and set me down on a radiator.

"Look kid, we have three rules at our school," the leader barked at me. "You don't swear" was the first rule he quoted. Now, I didn't really believe this rule given his behavior, but I thought that my best response probably wasn't, "Oh, don't worry I'm a preacher's kid, I would never think of swearing" so instead I just said, "OK." He went on to list the next rule, "And we don't spit." Again, I found the rule to be unusual, but just nodded my head. Then he and his comrades each broke out in a huge grin and gave me the third rule, "And we don't sit in spit." At that point, I realized that the back of my jeans were wet. To my horror I quickly realized that they had all spit on the radiator before sitting me on it. I also realized that an entire mob had grown to surround me and had witnessed the entire event. As kids can often do in these types of situations, cruelty won over compassion and they started laughing. With tears in my eyes, I ran to the bathroom and started cleaning the spit of three strangers off of my jeans. That cruelty continued for years at that school.

Why did those kids feel the need to shame me in front of the other kids? I questioned that for years. You see, there were other new kids that were left alone and not harassed. Sometimes it was because of their size. Sometimes it was not. It seemed to have more to do with their attitude. I have come to believe that part (just part) of why those kids did that to me was because I invited it. There was something in my demeanor and attitude that said, "I deserve to be treated badly." I invited that abuse and then I was shocked to receive it. Please hear me when I say that not all abuse is done because we invite it. And I am *definitely* not excusing the abuser for the behavior. However, I am trying to empower each of us to take control over anything that we may be contributing to the problem. My life changed when I quit inviting people to treat me badly. My life improved when I started to expect people to treat me with the same amount of respect I was willing to give to them. My life gained joy as I built confidence in my worthiness as a human being to live with dignity and self-respect. That doesn't mean that no one will ever mistreat me again. What it does mean is that (despite brief lapses here and there), I will never *invite* them to be cruel to me. And maybe it works just like those old vampire movies. Maybe the bloodsucker cannot enter the house unless you invite him in.

In addition to inviting people to mistreat us, irrational thoughts can make us panic in the face of conflict, which often causes us to avoid dealing with the conflict. This type of irrational thinking can take many forms, including:

- If I say anything, she will be mad at me.
- I'll get fired if I bring up the subject to him.
- Nothing that I can say will make a difference so it is not worth it.

- Something bad will happen if I confront her.
- It will absolutely crush him if I tell him how I really feel.

These are just some examples of how this irrational thinking can form in our heads. Whenever we exaggerate the consequences of dealing with conflict, then we do ourselves a disservice. In my experience coaching many conflict cowards, these thoughts are often unrealistic, and the imagined consequences are frequently just that—imagined rather than real. The TruthTalk system that we will cover in the next chapter will help you determine that.

The third way irrational thoughts can impact conflict situations is that the thoughts can actually cause people to get upset when there is nothing to be upset about. Have you ever had someone mad at you who was mad just because they misunderstood something you said or did? This happens all of the time. The person is reacting to their perception or interpretation of what you did rather than to your actual behavior! For example, I once worked with an executive who was furious with one of his colleagues from a different office who did not show up for an important meeting and then did not return several phone calls. During our coaching session my client was furious. He talked about how he never did fully trust this individual and how his true stripes were showing from his obvious sabotage of the meeting and his lack of responsiveness in returning his phone calls. My client was venting about how he was going to deal with this individual and had started a fairly elaborate plan of protection and attack. At this point his assistant interrupted our phone call. The assistant informed my client that his manager had called to let him know that the colleague who missed the meeting had been in a car accident the day before. My client's colleague was actually hospitalized, and the manager had told him that he would take care of everything. However, the meeting had slipped the manager's mind and he was calling to apologize to my client. My client felt very embarrassed as he got back on the line and explained all of this to me. The whole injustice had been manufactured in his mind. His colleague had done nothing wrong, and yet he had expended great mental energy in playing out his whole imagined scenario in his mind. This example was dramatic, but the concept of self-created negative emotions based on assumptions happens at some level for most of us on a weekly (or even daily) basis. How unfortunate that many would choose to live their lives getting upset over things that are not even fully true.

The fourth way that irrational thinking can impact conflict comes when there really is something that would be truly upsetting to most people. However, the problem comes when we worsen the conflict by exaggerating our level of emotional reaction. When we review the TruthTalk system for changing irrational thoughts, you will see that this is not an approach meant to get rid of emotions. I love emotion and would hate to live without it. There are times that you should be upset, angry, frustrated, sad, etc. However, if you are like me then you want to strive to make sure your feelings are based on reality and truth rather than exaggerations of reality. For example, it is perfectly sane to be frustrated and disappointed when you do not get a raise that you were hoping for. However, it is not usually a sane response to turn this disappointment into a huge injustice. The level of anger experienced by some people over minor issues can be dramatic. You don't need to look any further than driving a car to understand what I mean. Have you ever accidentally pulled out in front of someone going too slowly only to have them create an even more dangerous situation by tailgating you and then blowing past you yelling and shaking their fist? The action was accidental. The offense was minor. And yet the reaction was intense. Many conflicts are caused when people exaggerate the emotional reaction to the mistake. We then in turn tend to react to their reaction rather than to the core issue. These exaggerated emotions can lead both parties to do and say things that they will later regret.

Hopefully, I have presented a credible case for how irrational beliefs and reactions can impact us to conflict. While you cannot always have control over someone else who is being irrational (but we do have techniques that can help in later chapters), you can have control over your own emotional response. You can have this control if you *choose* to have this control. I will show you how in chapter 18.

Exercises
Self-reflection exercise: Examining your own irrational beliefs
Examine the last three times that you were overly upset in a conflict situation.

What were you saying to yourself that caused the emotion? Keep asking your-self what the core belief was that caused you to get so upset. Then pick the cat-egory that best fits your irrational thinking. Use the chart below to track at least three of these occasions.

	Situation #1	Situation #2	Situation #3
Record the facts about the situation that upset you.			
What did you feel?			
What were you saying to your-self that upset you? What core beliefs played a role?			
Which of the four categories does your thinking fall into? Circle all that apply.	Inviting the problem Panic at the thought of conflict Getting upset at nothing Exaggerating my emotions	Inviting the problem Panic at the thought of conflict Getting upset at nothing Exaggerating my emotions	Inviting the problem Panic at the thought of conflict Getting upset at nothing Exaggerating my emotions

Self-reflection exercise: Common core beliefs

What are your common core beliefs? Below you will find a list of irrational beliefs that are common to the American culture. Many of these were adapted from the work of the founder of rational emotive therapy, Albert Ellis. I have added other beliefs that are specifically related to conflict that I have found to be common with my coaching clients. Circle any of the beliefs below with which you struggle.

General irrational thoughts

- I must prove myself as adequate or competent.
- I must have love and approval almost all the time from significant people in my life.
- People who do misdeeds are bad and should be severely punished.
- Life is awful when things do not go the way I want them to.
- My problems come from others and I don't have the ability to change them.
- If I am afraid of something then I must stay preoccupied with it.
- It is easier to avoid difficulties than to show self-discipline and deal with them.
- My past determines how I act today.
- It is awful when I do not find good solutions to life's hassles.
- I can find happiness by being passive.
- I must have a high degree of order and certainty in order to feel comfortable.
- My general worth is determined by my performance and what people think of me.

Irrational thoughts specific to conflict

- It would be terrible if I were to lose a relationship because of conflict.
- In a conflict situation I won't be able to control what I say.
- It is possible not to have conflict with others.
- Conflict always has bad results.

- I don't deserve to be treated with respect.
- Conflict is not worth it because I am powerless to change the situation.
- Conflict is bad.
- This is just the way I am and I can't change the way I handle conflict.
- The other person is the one who should change. I shouldn't have to work at this.
- I couldn't stand it if someone thought less of me in a conflict.
- If I avoid the conflict, it will go away.
- It is always better to avoid conflict than to face it.

Now go back and review the thoughts that you circled and answer the following questions:

When you take your emotions out of these statements, do you really believe them? Are they based on fact or on emotion?

Are these beliefs that you teach to your friends, children, colleagues, etc., as true for them? If not, what does that suggest?

Where did you learn to believe each of these?

How committed are you to change these beliefs and learn new beliefs based more on truth than interpretation?

Next steps and additional resources

Talk to some people who seem to deal with conflict well. Show them the list of irrational beliefs. Ask them what they believe and why. Take the time to really explore this with them. See what you can learn from their perspectives and beliefs. Ask them for support as you attempt to change the way that you think when you deal with conflict. Then get ready to learn how to change these beliefs by going to chapter 18.

For more on cognitive approaches to irrational thinking, try *A New Guide to Rational Living* by Albert Ellis, Ph.D., and Robert Harper, Ph.D.

> *"The most immutable barrier in nature is between one man's thoughts and another's."*
>
> —William James

> *"Common sense is the collection of prejudices acquired by age eighteen."*
>
> —Albert Einstein

You've Got the Tools, You've Got the Talent: Techniques to Handle Any Conflict

Chapter 18:

The Truth and Nothing But the Truth: Using TruthTalk

So now you know that you as well as everyone else on this planet walks around thinking irrational thoughts. Some people (a minority) can change their irrational thinking just by identifying it. However, most of us need a structure to truly change these destructive thoughts. In this chapter you will learn TruthTalk, a strategy built on the foundations of cognitive therapy. With this step-by-step approach, you will learn how to conquer irrational thoughts and replace them with thoughts that help you rather than hurt you. Given the option between thinking thoughts that help and thoughts that hurt, is there really a choice?

Real life

Let's look at two real life stories of individuals with opposite styles when it comes to conflict and see how TruthTalk helped each of them change.

Example #1: Never good enough

When John was twelve years old, he ran home in delight to tell his parents that he had won second place in an important band competition. He was full of joy and excitement and appropriate pride in himself. As he burst through the front door with his chest puffed out and his head held high, he yelled out for his parents. His mother was the first to arrive, but as he started to explain his triumph to her, she interrupted him and yelled at him for tracking dirt in the house. He tried to explain again, but she cut him off, telling him to take off his dirty shoes and curtly added that she didn't have time to talk because she was making dinner. Deflated but not defeated, John rushed to find his father to tell him about his accomplishment. He found his dad in front of the television with a beer in his hand as usual. John proudly burst out his good news to his father. Without looking away from the television screen, his father simply replied, "Second place is for losers. Bother me when you get first." With his head hung low in shame, John went to his room. Behind a locked door, he vowed to himself that he would never celebrate anything again unless he was number one.

I didn't meet John until three decades after this incident. He came to coaching because of stress at work. John was an incredible performer who had an unpredictable temper. While his individual work was outstanding, he did not handle differences with others well at all. In fact, many people felt like John had only an off-on switch when it came to his opinion; either he didn't seem to have one (or didn't care) or he had to have it his way. Because of his high performance track record, John had been promoted many times over. When I met him, he had been in a senior executive position for about two years. However, John's boss was running out of patience, and John was being told that the company would replace him if he didn't improve how he dealt with the people that he was managing. I reviewed John's 360 degree feedback report with him, and people were saying the following:

- John expects perfection from others and is demeaning when things are not done to his standards.
- John micromanages his team.
- John does not delegate well.
- John does not listen to others who have different opinions than him.
- John's first reaction to conflict is to "draw a line in the sand" and warn others not to cross it.
- John refuses to help team members work out conflict. Instead he tells them to work it out themselves "or else."

John was devastated. He told me he had never failed anything in his whole life, but he just didn't know what to do. John was not a bad man. John was a man who was controlled by irrational thoughts.

Example Life #2: Anger and conflict are bad, bad, bad.

"So what happened growing up when you showed that you were angry?" was my question to Samantha. Sam was a CEO of a thirty million-dollar company. She had started the company from nothing and had turned her hobby into a highly successful business. Samantha called me for some coaching because, despite her great financial success, she found that she was not happy. As the company grew, so did the size of her staff. As the size of her staff grew, so did the number of conflictual situations. Like many entrepreneurs, Samantha still had her hands in all parts of the business and was trying to be all things to all people. She had not built a strong senior management team, and therefore many squabbles between workers and departments ended up at her door.

When we started our coaching relationship, Samantha and I talked of a dual approach to her challenges. We were going to work on helping her become a true CEO and structure her company in a way that made best use of her talents. That involved training her staff, hiring new people, and changing policies and habits that encouraged conflicts to show up in her office. However, besides that practical business approach, Samantha also wanted to understand why she hated conflict so much. She confided with me that her conflict patterns impacted all areas of her life, including her marriage and her relationship with her children. Therefore, we spent some time reviewing her beliefs concerning conflict. She shared with me that she grew up in a chaotic environment with her two parents and an older brother. Our conversation went something like this:

> TIM: So what happened growing up when you showed that you were angry?

> SAM: I don't think that I ever showed anger growing up.

> TIM: Anger is a pretty normal emotion that most children feel growing up. Many learn lessons early on about the rules of conflict from how their parents react when they show frustration and anger. What did your parents do when your older brother showed anger?

SAM: Well, I learned from his mistakes, let me tell you. He and my mom were constantly fighting. They would bicker back and forth until my dad finally came in the room and would put an end to it.

TIM: How did he put an end to it?

SAM: Different ways at different times. When my brother was younger, he would just scream at him and talk about how it was his house and his rules and if my brother didn't like it then he should just get out. When my brother got older, he and Dad got into it physically. I'll never forget the night that my brother actually pushed my father down to the ground. Mom and Dad kicked him out of the house that night and my brother went to live with our uncle. My brother never came back to live with us. He and my parents don't talk much to each other even now, except a little on holidays.

TIM: That sounds pretty intense, Samantha. What kind of impact do you think that had on you at the time?

SAM: Well, I had learned even before then that anger was a big no-no around the house. I mean, all of this started because of how my mom handled my brother when he was upset. The fights never started with my brother and dad. Dad would just come in and take care of it when Mom would get upset enough.

TIM: What was your mother's initial reaction to your brother's anger?

SAM: Mom was funny. I mean, it was like she would do anything for you, and I think she really loved us.

But there were hidden rules, like the fact that you had to *really* notice how much she was giving to you and you could *never* be upset with her. She was giving, but she was always right.

TIM: *So, how did these rules play out when your brother was upset?*

SAM: Oh, Mom would turn on a dime. She might be completely happy, but if he showed frustration or anger, she would turn on him completely and start defending herself and criticizing him. Then my brother would get even more upset, and it would escalate until Dad came in, and we know what happened then.

TIM: *Given that you're five years younger than your brother, you got to watch and learn from this experience. So what was your learning?*

SAM: I think I learned that it was a lot safer to keep your anger to yourself. I mean, nobody handled it well. It's probably why I had an ulcer at eleven years old.

TIM: *What do you think happens internally when you have all of these employees coming to you with their anger?*

SAM: It drives me absolutely crazy! I get all tensed up inside and I start panicking like something bad is going to happen. I then find myself trying to appease everyone, and they often end up feeling better while I feel completely drained and nervous. I mean, I'm a CEO of a huge company and I am very successful, but when this happens I feel like that eleven-year-old again.

How it applies

Both have difficulty dealing with conflict, yet, their difficulties are different from one another in several ways. John is aggressive with conflict. He is either not in conflict or is in it with both barrels firing. Samantha is a more traditional conflict coward. She thinks conflict is bad and does not want to deal with it. Another difference evident in their stories is that Samantha's conflict behavior came directly from her reaction to how others dealt with conflict in her life growing up. John's conflict behavior is more subtly related to his view of himself and expectations. We will explore both of these situations later in this chapter using the strategy of TruthTalk.

TruthTalk owes its existence to a number of cognitive-behavioral theories that have explored the fact that how we talk to ourselves has a dramatic impact on our feelings and behaviors. Our perceptions become our reality. As some people read the above stories, they may be tempted to tell John and Samantha to "just get over it." I have always found it amazing that we would never expect someone to be a top athlete the first time they realized how to dribble a basketball, but we expect one insight into our psyche to instantaneously change the way we have been feeling and behaving for most of our lives!

Even clients I work with often want all of their problems to go away because they realized where they come from. Unfortunately, it is not that simple. Imagine that you have spent thirty years subconsciously saying to yourself, "I'm a failure." Thirty years of beating yourself up for every single mistake that you make. Then, after thirty years, you finally realize that you feel like a failure because of patterns from your childhood. Do you really think that all of the sudden you won't feel like a failure anymore? Don't get me wrong, insight is great and often needed as a first step toward change, but it is not the only step toward change. Some people spend the rest of their lives defending the way they think, feel, and behave because of a past offense against them. It is true that the people who hurt you are responsible for what they did. However, it is equally true that no matter what they did, you are responsible for how you live now. They don't have the power to change you, only you do. Insight, while helpful, is often not the full solution.

In addition to offenses done against us, we also have to deal with the offenses we have perpetuated inside our heads—the habit of negative self-talk. Having a structure to combat these thoughts is crucial for long-term success. Having fair expectations is crucial for really changing old habits (i.e., don't expect to defeat thirty years of saying, "I'm a failure," with two weeks of saying, "I'm a success"). To truly beat habitual irrational thoughts, you must have dedication and tenacity. So, with insight, structure, fair expectations, and tenacity, you can diminish irrational thoughts in both intensity and duration and live a happier and more peaceful life without all of the useless mind traffic that irrational thoughts create. Let's take a look at how this applies to one of our real-life stories.

John's core irrational thinking habits were solidified the day that his mother and father did not recognize his accomplishments. As John and I talked, it was apparent that several people in his present life did recognize his accomplishments. He had a supportive wife who praised him and he had bosses who, in the past, thought he could do no wrong. However, all of that praise could not get past John's mental barriers. He always thought that whatever he did was not good enough. He always compared himself to someone who was doing better in some way. When John started managing people, this feeling got worse. Now he had even less control over his performance because part of his performance was judged on how *other* people behaved. Therefore, whenever someone had a different opinion than John or did something different than how he would do it, he would react poorly.

When John was not in control, his fear of failure would increase and he would react with tension and anger, like a fearful, cornered animal. Others just viewed this behavior as stubborn and rigid. They did not know that it was based in fear. Paradoxically, John's fear of failure was actually causing him to behave in a way that increased his chances for failure. Fortunately, John was able to change his mindset using the TruthTalk strategy. Before we go into detail on how he changed, we need to discuss the TruthTalk Thought Tracking Form.

In the previous chapter I used a chart to help you start tracking your self-talk. It looked like this:

	Situation
Record the facts about the situation that upset you.	
What did you feel?	
What were you saying to yourself that upset you or what core beliefs played a role?	
Which of the four categories does your thinking fall into? Circle all that apply.	Inviting the problem Panic at the thought of conflict Getting upset at nothing Exaggerating my emotions

The last row that explored the categories was mainly for your insight from the last chapter. The full TruthTalk tracking system eliminates this section because TruthTalk can be applied to any area of irrational thinking, not just with conflict. Therefore, the chart looks like this:

TruthTalk Thought Changing Form

The Catalyst for Your Reaction (What *happened?* Record the facts about the situation that upset you.)	
Mindset (What were you *saying* to yourself that upset you? What core beliefs played a role?)	

Feelings (How did you *feel* about the event?)	
Behavior (What did you *do* in response to the event?)	
Truth Test (Is what you are saying about the event *completely* true?)	
Strategic Test (Is your mental response to the event *helping* or *hurting* you?)	
New Mindset (What is a truthful, but *more helpful* mindset in response to the event?)	
The Productive Response (How could you respond to this event in a way that would be even more *productive?*)	
The Opportunity Challenge (What are some *positive* results that are possible from this event?)	

Let's break down the system.

The catalyst for your reaction

The first row asks the participant to simply record an event that was the catalyst for the feeling or reaction that you would like to change. The important thing to remember about recording the catalyst for your mindset is to make sure you just record the facts. For example, "My boss raised her voice at me today," could be presented as a fact. "My boss is a jerk" is not a fact, but rather an interpretation of the situation. What she did may be seen by some people as "jerky," but others may not see it that way. In addition, how many jerky things does someone have to do before they officially become a jerk? One, six, thirteen, more? There is no agreed upon system for this labeling. The catalyst has to be written as though you were an impartial observer to the situation.

Mindset

Row two looks at your mindset. As we discussed in the previous chapter, it is not what happens to us that causes our feelings, but how we interpret what happens to us. Your mindset is crucial in how you react to situations and will steer you to a positive or negative direction. There are several ways to discover what your mindset is. Think about what you are saying to yourself that is upsetting you. How are you interpreting the event/catalyst that occurred? What closely held beliefs may be impacting your reaction to the situation?

At times, clients try to put questions in the mindset section of the thought tracking form. I discourage against this because it is much more tangible to deal with statements than questions. Behind every question that creates a negative emotion is a feared negative statement. For example, if you look at yourself in the mirror and ask yourself, "Do I look fat in these jeans?" and end up feeling sad, then what are you really thinking? That's right, you are thinking, "I look fat in these jeans." If you were thinking, "Woo-woo, I look great!" then you would not be feeling sad. If you are considering confronting someone and you are thinking, "I wonder if he will get mad," and you find yourself afraid, then what is really going on inside? Likely, you are either thinking, "He might get mad," or, "He will get mad at me." Any question that creates negative emotions will always have a potential negative statement beneath it. Some more examples:

Question	Possible statement beneath the question
Does he really love me?	He doesn't love me (or he might not love me).
Will they ever get here?	They are going to be incredibly late.
Did I do a good job?	I might have done a lousy job.
Will he ever shut up?	I can't stand listening to him.
How is she going to react?	She is going to hate what I have to say.

Therefore, anytime you find yourself writing a question in the mindset section, simply ask yourself, "How am I answering this question internally that is causing me to be upset?"

At times, people will argue that their reactions are so immediate that they are not thinking anything, but rather are just feeling upset. To them I would argue that our thoughts are lightening fast and subconscious at times. So on many of these occasions (perhaps not all), you are still thinking something in response to the event that is upsetting you.

Feelings

The third row of the TruthTalk system is focused on your emotional reaction. What did you feel in response to your self-talk about the event? What were your emotional reactions? At times my clients who are less emotionally aware try to put a thought in this section (this is especially true for men who think that hunger is a primary emotion). Some examples of emotions:

Happiness	Sadness
Anger	Embarrassment
Shame	Guilt
Fear	Hesitation
Concern	Terror
Helplessness	Despair

This third row simply gives you insight into what you are feeling. Some clients of mine prefer to record their emotional reaction before recording their mindset. Sometimes they are more aware of what they are feeling than what they are thinking. After identifying their emotions, it helps them to figure out, "What must I be saying to myself to cause me to feel that way?"

Behavior

The next section in the TruthTalk formula is to record your behavior in response to the catalyst. We have looked at what you were thinking and what you were feeling, now we want to look at what you were doing. What actions did you take in response to the event? Did you avoid, yell at someone, kick the dog, or something else? Focus specifically on behaviors that may not have been useful to you.

The truth test and strategic test

Now it's time to put your thoughts and reactions to the test. The fifth and sixth rows in the thought-tracking form present two methods for testing whether your thoughts are rational or irrational. The first test is the truth test. Is what you are saying to yourself completely true? Can you prove it? If the thought is not 100 percent true and/or you can't prove it, then it seems pretty irrational to keep saying it to yourself. Wouldn't it be better to tell yourself the truth rather than lies or partial lies? Why in the world would you want to keep saying something to yourself that may not be true?

The second test is the strategic test. Are your thoughts helping or hurting you? Ask yourself, "How well do my thoughts serve me?" Isn't it incredibly self-defeating and irrational to keep saying things to yourself that aren't helpful? Wouldn't your life be better if you just said true things to yourself that helped you? As I mentioned in the previous chapter, I am not a big fan of overly positive thinking. Some schools of thought have you saying things to yourself that just are not true (e.g., "I'm the number one salesperson in the company" when you are really way down on the ladder). If that kind of approach works for you, then keep it up. In my experience, most people have an issue with that type of self-talk because it simply isn't true. In TruthTalk, we do focus on saying positive thoughts, *but* we base these thoughts on the truth. This leads us to the next section in the system.

The new mindset

In the seventh row of the TruthTalk form you are asked to create new self-statements. You only follow this step if your previous thoughts are either not completely true or do not help you. If your mindset fails either of these tests, then fill out the new thought section. The key here is to find a new statement that is both true and helpful; a thought that moves you toward your goals rather than away from them. One way to do this is to pretend that you are on a debate team and that the other side is defending the old mindset. Your goal is to debate the old mindset, to come up with contrary evidence, and to present a different perspective. To be successful, you must attack the old negative thought with great determination. For example, let's say that you are avoiding telling your spouse about something he did that you did not like. The old mindset that is keeping you from telling him is, "I can't stand it when he gets upset with me." Here are some possible ways to debate that thought:

- It's true that I don't like it when he is upset, but it will not destroy me.
- I don't even know if he is going to be upset, and if he is I can handle it.
- I'm going to tell him that I am upset because it is the right thing to do.
- It is better to just tell him what I feel instead of trying to guess at his reaction.
- As long as he is not demeaning, he has the right to be upset if that is what he feels.
- In order for our relationship to be close, I need to tell him how I feel.
- I will never like it when people are upset with me, but I am a strong and capable person and I will speak my mind with respect and truth.

These are just a few examples of more powerful mindsets that will lead to positive action rather than avoidance or negative behavior.

The productive response

The next row encourages you to create a productive response. In this section we are looking at behavior rather than just feelings and thoughts. Look for alternatives to the behavior you were showing in response to the old mindset. Look for ways to create actions that improve your life and help you grow. In our example with the potentially upset spouse, the action might be to set a time to talk to your spouse about what is bothering you. Because your mindset and emotions are calmer, you have a greater chance of doing this in a way that will be helpful and productive rather than making the problem worse.

The opportunity challenge

The final row of the TruthTalk form goes beyond merely repairing the negative mindsets. This section encourages you to look for the opportunity challenge hidden in the problem. This section requires creativity and thoughtfulness, but can be very exciting when you see the great possibilities that were not apparent to you before. Allow yourself to think outside of the box and see how you can turn this challenge into an opportunity.

Now that I have walked you through each of the sections, let's return to John's story. I used the TruthTalk formula with John and here is one example of an event we worked through using the system:

TruthTalk Thought Changing Form—John

The Catalyst for Your Reaction (What *happened?* Record the facts about the situation that upset you.)	A person that I manage turned in a report to me that had an obvious mistake about one of the company's procedures.
Mindset (What were you *saying* to yourself that upset you? What core beliefs played a role?)	I will never make our department #1 with this kind of sloppy work. Nothing ever gets done right unless I do it myself. I'll never be successful.

Feelings (How did you *feel* about the event?)	Fear and anger
Behavior (What did you *do* in response to the event?)	Spent a half-hour rewriting the report. Called the person in my office and let her have it for causing me the extra frustration and work.
Truth Test (Is what you are saying about the event *completely* true?)	No. I was exaggerating the problem. The people I manage do get many things right. The truth is that I won't succeed by doing things myself. This one error will not make or break my chances for success.
Strategic Test (Is your response to the event *helping* or *hurting* you?)	My response was hurting me because it was leading me back to old habits. I was too rough on the person and I did not benefit anyone by doing the work myself.
New Mindset (What is a truthful, but *more helpful* mindset in response to the event?)	It is frustrating when people don't catch mistakes, but it is not the end of the world. Anyone can make a mistake, and it is my job as a manager to use this as a learning experience for her. I want to give her feedback in a way that helps her grow and builds our relationship.

The Productive Response (How could you respond to this event in a way that would be even more *productive?*)	It would have been better to respectfully educate her on the mistake and put her on the task to research it and rewrite the report. I will apologize to her for my anger and commit to more productive behavior for next time.
The Opportunity Challenge (What are some *positive* results that are possible from this event?)	This is a chance to break free of my tendency to do everything myself and learn to build a member of my team to be more knowledgeable and productive.

Notice that these thoughts came from one event. To make full use of TruthTalk, you need to do this system for multiple events. Over time, you will notice emerging patterns of certain irrational thoughts. In my work I have found that most people have three to seven core irrational thoughts specific to their difficulties. Once you discover what these are and discipline yourself to combat them, you will have greater peace and satisfaction.

Going back to the four factors necessary to change John's thought process we see the following:

Insight: John learned that his perfectionism originated with his reaction to how his parent's handled his accomplishments.

Structure: John submitted his thinking to the TruthTalk process and was diligent in following the structure.

Fair expectations: John accepted that insight alone was unlikely to change his irrational thinking. He embraced the fact that it would take time, effort, and practice to make true changes.

Tenacity: John kept with the system working over months to make the rational thoughts more habitual.

The results of months of working on this thought patterns were dramatic. John kept his job. His feedback from those he managed improved dramatically.

And believe it or not, his performance actually increased rather than decreased when he no longer expected perfection from himself or others.

Exercises
Knowledge Challenge: Samantha's TruthTalk

Do the TruthTalk form for Samantha (our other example at the start of this chapter). I have filled in a few bits of information. See how you do with the rest. After you have attempted this, take a look at the completed form in the appendix.

TruthTalk Thought-Changing Form—Samantha

The Catalyst for Your Reaction (What *happened?* Record the facts about the situation that upset you.)	One of Samantha's managers came in to her office complaining about one of the other managers.
Mindset (What were you *saying* to yourself that upset you? What core beliefs played a role?)	Samantha thought to herself, "Here we go again. They can't ever resolve these things themselves. If I don't calm the situation down then someone is going to quit."
Feelings (How did you *feel* about the event?)	Samantha felt apprehensive, concerned, and angry.
Behavior (What did you *do* in response to the event?)	Samantha tried to calm the manager down and empathized greatly with his feelings. She then went to the other manager and calmed her down and empathized with her. She asked both of them to let it go and support one another.

Truth Test (Is what you are saying about the event *completely* true?)	
Strategic Test (Is your response to the event *helping* or *hurting* you?)	
New Mindset (What is a truthful, but *more helpful* mindset in response to the event?)	
The Productive Response (How could you respond to this event in a way that would be even more *productive*?)	
The Opportunity Challenge (What are some *positive* results that are possible from this event?)	

Application exercise: Your TruthTalk

Pick a recent conflict situation that upset you. Walk yourself through the TruthTalk process below:

TruthTalk Thought-Changing Form—You

The Catalyst for Your Reaction (What *happened?* Record the facts about the situation that upset you.)	

Mindset (What were you *saying* to yourself that upset you? What core beliefs played a role?)	
Feelings (How did you *feel* about the event?)	
Behavior (What did you *do* in response to the event?)	
Truth Test (Is what you are saying about the event *completely* true?)	
Strategic Test (Is your response to the event *helping* or *hurting* you?)	
New Mindset (What is a truthful, but *more helpful* mindset in response to the event?)	
The Productive Response (How could you respond to this event in a way that would be even more *productive?*)	

The Opportunity Challenge (What are some *positive* results that are possible from this event?)	

Next steps and additional resources

In the appendix you will find a blank TruthTalk form. Feel free to make photocopies of this form for your personal use. Spend time each week tracking your thoughts and applying the TruthTalk process to them. With practice, see if you can discover your core irrational thoughts. When you discover these, put your powerful new mindsets on index cards and read them daily for at least one month. Then use these index cards whenever the old way of thinking tries to grab you. Refuse to believe the lies of the past, and commit yourself to saying the truth to yourself—the truth and nothing but the truth!

For another resource on combating negative thoughts, try *Ten Days to Self-Esteem* by David D. Burns, M.D.

"Man must cease attributing his problems to his environment, and learn again to exercise his will—his personal responsibility."
—Albert Schweitzer

"Finally, brothers, whatever is true, whatever is pure, whatever is lovely, whatever is admirable—if anything is excellent or praiseworthy—think about such things."
—Philippians 4:8

"You cannot always control what goes on outside. But you can always control what goes on inside."
—Wayne Dyer

Chapter 19:

The Relationship between Wants, Fairness, and Integrity

There are many levels to communication. In this chapter we will look at three of these levels; sharing your feelings, determining fairness, and communicating and making decisions out of integrity. By learning to separate these levels, you can have better conversations around difficult topics and greater resolution of differences.

Real life

My wife and I were very excited as we drove from Columbus, Ohio, to De Kalb, Illinois, to look for an apartment. I had been accepted to graduate school in De Kalb, which was my excitement, and Marla had the opportunity to move away from Ohio, which was hers! The drive took us approximately eight hours during a time when the speed limit was 55 miles per hour. Now, at that time in my life I took the speed limit very seriously (can anyone find the hidden confession in this sentence?). To me there was a reason that they called it the speed *limit* and that meant that I would not drive over 55. I was a law-abiding citizen when it came to speeding and felt proud of my discipline.

Once we got to De Kalb, we started frantically looking for an apartment, not knowing anyone, not sure where we were going, and not familiar with the surroundings, including certain speed zones areas (can you sense the foreshadowing here?). De Kalb had cornfields in town, as well as out of town, which explains how a law-abiding citizen such as myself happened to be going 45 in a 35-mile per hour zone.

As soon as I noticed the speed limit sign, I slowed down to 35 miles per hour, but the flashing red lights behind me told me that it was too late. "No problem," I thought as I quickly planned my speech to the officer to help him understand this unfortunate misunderstanding. However, the interaction did not go as I planned.

After being rudely greeted with the standard, "Do you realize how fast you were going?" question, I quickly began to tell the officer my story. With great detail I talked about our need to find an apartment, the 55-mile per hour marathon from Ohio, and, of course, the whole De Kalb cornfields confusion. With all of this said, I felt confident that the officer would simply release me with a stiff verbal warning. I was wrong.

I was getting a little worried when he took my driver's license back to the squad car and waited for some amount of time. He returned to my car frowning. "I'm afraid that I can't accept your license as bond in Illinois, you'll have to come to the station and post fifty dollars bail," he said without any sign of remorse.

Now, this was bad for several reasons. Number one, my wife and I were broke and did not have fifty dollars. Number two, having cornfields in town was entrapment in my book. Third and finally, I had just driven 55 miles per hour for eight hours and it was unfair for me to get a ticket (at least in my mind). I was very confident of my ability to get this officer to see how going to jail right now just didn't fit into my schedule. Wrong again!

The officer asked me to get out of the car and come back to the squad car. So I tried once again to show him the error of his judgment and change his mind. Our conversation continued on for a few more minutes as he insisted on taking me into the police station and I insisted that I did not have the time. It did not seem fair to me, especially in light of my having obeyed the speed limit for the previous eight hours when I would have much rather been speeding. Eventually, he ordered me out of the car and put me against my door in order to frisk me. "Why are you frisking me?" I asked out of confusion and disbelief as cars slowly passed us with drivers forming their own hypotheses of my crime. At this point he threatened to handcuff me if I did not shut up. Marla asked, "What should I do?" Checking with the officer for permission as to not risk escalating my plight, I told her, "Well, I guess go check out the apartment and then come visit me at the slammer and we'll figure out what to do."

So that is what she did. Marla went to the apartment and I went to the jail. Fortunately, by the time we got to the jail, I had filled the officer's head with enough stories of my internship in the social services division of a police department to convince him that I was not a dangerous criminal. However, "rules are rules," so I used my one phone call to try to contact Marla's parents and ask them to wire us some money. I then patiently waited and tried to resist the temptation to start singing "Nobody Knows the Trouble I've Seen."

In the meantime, Marla went to the apartment and, despite liking it, was somehow not able to put aside the fact that her husband was "doing hard time" at the moment. She later told me that she started crying in front of the couple who were showing her the apartment. When they asked her what was wrong, the only thing that she could get out of her mouth was, "My...husband's...in...jail."

Well, needless to say, I got out of jail, but for some strange reason the landlords didn't want to rent us that apartment. The lesson that I learned, however, was about fairness. Fairness is in the eye of the beholder.

How it applies

To the officer, I deserved a ticket because I broke the law, which was fair. To me, I deserved a break since the speeding was completely accidental and I had obeyed the law for the entire trip. Fairness was in the eye of the beholder. You don't need to look too deeply in any relationship to see the *very* subjective nature of fairness. We have a very difficult time separating out what we want and what we feel from what is fair.

This challenge of honestly assessing fairness is true for all relationships, both at work and in our personal lives. To communicate effectively, we need to know how to talk about wants separate from fairness. And often we need to go beyond fairness to a higher level of integrity. Effective conflict resolution involves three elements that build upon each other; sharing wants, focusing on fairness, and responding with integrity.

Many individuals who avoid conflict don't even do the first step; they never tell the other person how they feel or what they want. To speak your heart and mind requires knowing yourself and giving yourself the right to have opinions and desires. If you refuse to give yourself the right to ask for what you want (even when you are unsure if it is fair), then you are incapable of discussing fairness (the discussion will be lopsided in the other person's favor). When we negotiate fairness, we go beyond wants and try to understand the other person's perspective, which is impossible for the other person if you have not spoken your mind. However, fairness is not the ultimate destination. When my sons were five years old, the idea of what was fair and not fair ruled many of our discussions. Hopefully, as we grow up, we strive to move beyond a fairness perspective and respond with integrity (being who you are and who you want to be in the situation), even when it isn't fair. To deal effectively with conflict, you need to be able to walk yourself and the other person through each of these sequentially; sharing wants, focusing on fairness, and responding with integrity.

Sharing wants

As I mentioned earlier, if you are a conflict coward, you will often avoid telling the other person what you really want. There are many reasons for this tendency. Perhaps you have been "trained" to believe that you are not suppose to have wants (especially at work). Maybe you have had your spirit stifled by overbearing parents, spouses, or bosses. Or maybe you build up your fear of the other person's reaction, either being afraid of their anger or of the possibility of hurting their feelings. Whatever the reason, you are still the only person who can change the patterns because you hold the secret. Somewhere, deep down, you know what you want.

In any significant relationship, the sharing of wants is crucial. Sharing is necessary in order to build intimacy and resolve conflict. Sharing wants creates opportunities for compromise and helps the other person learn more about you. Sharing your wants challenges the person whom you are dealing with to change and grow. When you are ashamed to share what you feel and what you want, then your level of intimacy with the other person is highly limited. If you will not be genuine with your wants, then you may become bitter over the years of suppressing your feelings. The very conflicts you were trying to avoid become more hurtful than they would have been if you had dealt with them right away. You also do a disservice to others by not sharing your feelings because you are suppressing feedback that may help them improve their own behavior.

Focusing on fairness

Knowing and expressing wants is necessary for conflict resolution, but there is another essential step for dealing effectively with conflict. You must next be willing and able to discuss fairness. However, fairness (as in the case of my aforementioned speeding ticket) is in the eyes of the beholder. Most situations can be viewed from multiple angles. How we see fairness will be tainted by our past learning and experiences. We may defend, "Well, my friends agree with me," but the truth is that if we tell the story the right way, we can get others to agree with us fairly easily. It is not easy to truly see events through someone else's perspective. Truly, determining fairness is challenging because 100 percent fairness is not really possible.

Even though complete fairness is impossible, it is important to be able to discuss fairness in a relationship. Being able to discuss fairness and look at issues from someone else's point of view is an improvement over just being able to express your own feelings and wants. However, there is one more level of improvement that is much harder to achieve. That is learning how to deal with conflict by responding with honor and integrity.

Responding with honor and integrity

Living with integrity is not an easy task. While speaking wants and determining fairness have their challenges, integrity decisions are even more difficult. When I speak of integrity, I am referring to an unrelenting pursuit toward emotional, cognitive, and spiritual wholeness. Integrity can only be chosen if you are able to know what you want, speak your mind, and determine fairness, but it is far greater than any of these.

When you guard your integrity, you make decisions that represent the person you are striving to become rather than your automatic reactions, or even reactions that others may justify as a fair reaction to the situation. Integrity is not solely determined by behavior, but also by motivation. Integrity means that our desire to be the person we are striving to be outweighs the desire for the following:

- Justice
- To be right

- Fairness
- Self-protection

Have you ever noticed that in most movies it is not enough for the hero to act out of integrity and do the right thing? Justice has to occur. The bad guys have to be humiliated because it is not enough of a reward to act out of dignity. When things are not fair, it leaves a bad taste in our mouths. Now, I have nothing against fairness. I like it when things are fair. I'm just saying that when we focus more on fairness than integrity, we are cheating ourselves out of being the best people we can be.

Too many times, we approach relationships in a 50/50 manner. Unfortunately, this usually spells disaster. Relationships are based more on multiplication than addition. Therefore, if you have two people working at 50 percent, you have a relationship that is 25 percent as wonderful as it could be (.50 X .50 = .25). A relationship where one person is working at 100 percent and one is working at 50 percent is 50 percent as wonderful as it could be. Only with both people giving 100 percent can a relationship reach its full potential. The fantastic benefit of approaching relationships with honor and integrity is that instead of sinking down to the other person's level of behavior, you act as an inspiration to him and encourage him to act with more integrity. Most significant conflicts are not resolved until one person decides to act with integrity no matter what the other person does simply because that is who he wants to be!

Integrity's other role in conflict becomes evident when you have actually done something wrong and harmful. Have you hurt somebody who did not deserve it? Did you ever screw up something so badly that you feel that you don't even deserve to be forgiven? Have you ever begged for forgiveness from somebody only to have her deny you the healing flow that comes from being forgiven? I can answer all three of those questions with a resounding "yes" for myself. There is a specific time in my life when I let down a large number of people who were depending on me. I was not out to purposely hurt anyone, but my blindness to myself was so strong that I did hurt many people out of complete selfishness and pride. I'm fortunate that many, if not most of those people forgave me. Several did not, and two of the individuals whom I hurt the most, to my knowledge, have not forgiven me to this day.

I hate it. I hate the fact that I can't make it right. I use to daydream about having a time machine so that I could go back and fix the problem in myself, that I could do things differently and live with greater integrity. But I can't, and I never will be able to change what I did no matter how hard I pray, wish, or dream. But what I can do is to be sorry, to have conviction never to hurt anyone in that way again, and to try to give back to the world rather than just take from it.

Is there someone you have hurt either intentionally or unintentionally? Have you tried to make amends for what you did? Have you tried to tell him you are sorry? Have you been convinced in your heart that what you did was wrong and that you never want to do it again? If you have, then you have done all that you can. If you haven't, please try. I once was complaining to a colleague about the fact that there were people who had not forgiven me for what I had done, even though years had past. He kindly but forcefully put me in my place with one quote. He quoted Shakespeare who said, "Forgiveness to the injured, doth belong." It is not my right or your right to demand that others forgive us. That is their decision and their decision alone.

Therefore, I have accepted the fact that I may not be forgiven by everyone I hurt or offend on this planet. If it wasn't my fault, then I try not to care. If it was my fault, I care deeply, but try to respect their right to decide if they will ever forgive me.

Integrity takes many forms, and sometimes the form needs to be a humble apology to someone you have hurt. We all are human and we all will fail. When we do fail, the best we can do in response to our failure is try to respond with integrity. In other cases, we will decrease the conflict in our lives by building a practice of sharing wants, determining fairness, and acting with honor and integrity.

Exercises
Self-reflection exercise: Knowing your wants

If you have trouble stating what you feel or want, try the following. Stand in front of a mirror (yes, do it even if you feel goofy—I won't tell anyone). Look at yourself right in the eyes and tell that person in the mirror what you feel or what you want and why you want it. Own your feelings and wants by focusing on "I" statements like:

- I feel _____ when you _____ and I want you to _____.
- I'm not saying that this is necessarily rational or true, but I want to let you know that I felt _____ when _____ and I would feel better if you were to _____.
- I'm not saying that this is necessarily right or fair, but I want _____.
- What I really want out of this is _____.
- From my perspective _____.
- When I let myself dream about what I want out of life, the first thing that comes to mind is _____

Notice how you feel as you ask for your wants. Keep experimenting with this until you can state your wants with poise and confidence.

Interactive exercise: When others react poorly to you sharing wants

Some people are very sensitive to the reactions of others. If you are this type of individual, then this exercise is for you. Sometimes the person listening to you needs to be educated on how you respond to his or her reactions. Try using the following phrases to deal with a person who reacts poorly to you sharing what you want.

- I am trying to improve our relationship by sharing more with you about what I want. However, it feels hard for me to do this if you _____.
- I don't know if you realize it, but when I tell you what I want, it seems to me that you _____.
- It is really difficult for me to tell you what I want, so while I'm trying to improve in this, it would help me if you _____.

Self-reflection exercise: Determining fairness

If you have problems determining what is fair in a situation, ask yourself the following questions:

If my best friend were in this same situation that I am in, what rights would I give him or her?

If I was in the other person's shoes in this situation, what would I want?

Is there an answer to this situation that gives all involved what they want? If not, what is the closest solution?

Self-reflection exercise: Your personal integrity

Read the following and write the number that best corresponds with your behavior in the space allowed. Use the scale below for each statement:

1	2	3	4	5
Never	Rarely	Sometimes	Often	Always

My behavior toward others is consistent with the vision of who I want to be._____

I balance compassion and strength while interacting with others in conflictual situations._____

I am authentic with people in my personal life._____

I am authentic with people in my work life._____

I maintain my dignity with others when we have conflict._____

Becoming the person I want to be is more important to me than fairness and justice._____

My behavior towards others is consistent with my spiritual beliefs._____

I make sure I don't betray myself with my behavior toward others._____

Scoring

8-40: When we are talking about integrity we do not rest at anything under 100 percent despite our inability to ever achieve perfect integrity. Remember the pursuit of integrity should be unrelenting, so a score does not matter. We all are constantly striving.

Interactive exercise: Putting all three together

This exercise is best be done with a friend, coworker, or significant other who also has studied this chapter. When in the situation that shows potential conflict, do the following steps:

Step 1: Share what you want

Speak your thoughts, feelings, and desires with no regard to fairness or what your decision of integrity will be. Speak respectfully to the other person using opening phrases like "I feel...," "I think...," and "From my perspective..." The goal in this step is merely to be aware of your perspective and communicate it to the other person. Use what you have learned from this chapter to speak your heart and mind. Clarify in advance that you are not addressing what is fair yet; you are merely sharing what you want.

Step 2: Determine fairness

Look past your own perspective and try to understand the perspective of the other person. Summarize and reflect back to the other person what you think they are wanting or saying. Keep doing this until you are both sure that you understand each other. Then discuss any possible compromises to your two positions taking into account the issues that are driving both of your perspectives.

Step 3: Act with integrity

After sharing what you want, exploring the other person's position, and attempting to compromise, ask yourself the following questions:

In order to be the man or woman that I want to be, what do I need to do in this situation?

In order to be the whole person that I want to be, how do I need to react to this person?

Which is most important in this situation, fairness or integrity?

Step 4: Discuss your decision

Share with the other person your decision about the issue. If neither of you are able to take a position of integrity (or disagree about whether the decision is one of integrity), then agree to take the issue to a mediator for feedback and help.

Next steps and additional resources

Look for any examples of unresolved conflict in your life. Make an action plan on how you could go about using these principles to bring about closure with these conflicts. Look especially for instances when you allowed wants or fairness to rule over your integrity. Walk through each of the three levels of communication, looking at wants, fairness, and integrity.

Think of someone you have hurt. Write a letter to them without any justification, apologizing for how you have hurt them. Send the letter as an invitation for their forgiveness. Accept that it is their right whether they forgive you or not.

Think of someone who doesn't "deserve" to be forgiven by you, but who is sorry for what she did. Prayerfully consider giving them grace by writing a letter of forgiveness or acceptance.

To better understand grace from an evangelical perspective, read *In the Grip of Grace: You Can't Fall Beyond His Love* by Max Lucado. To explore the concept of honoring, try *Love Is a Decision: Thirteen Proven Principles to Energize Your Marriage and Family* by Gary Smalley and John Trent.

*"There is something immoral about abandoning
your own judgement."*
—Bruce Greenwood, playing JFK in the movie *Thirteen Days*

*"In the world to come, I shall not be asked, "Why were you not
Moses?" I shall be asked, "Why were you not Zusya?"*
—Rabbi Zusya

Chapter 20:

Assertiveness, Coward Style

Some people equate assertiveness with aggressiveness. Most conflict cowards despise aggression and thus may never try to develop their own form of assertiveness. Fortunately, true assertiveness does not have to be aggressive, and each individual can find his or her own style of assertiveness that feels right. In this chapter we will define the difference between passive, assertive, and aggressive responses, as well as look at different options available to help develop your own assertive style.

Real life

I looked at my clock and couldn't believe that it was 3:00 in the morning. It must have been the smell that woke me up. As my mind slowly gained some semblance of thought, I interpreted the smell as a possible gas leak. However, I carefully weighed the risk of being blown to smithereens versus the option of walking down into the stone cold basement to check the smell and quickly decided to go back to bed.

I woke up the next morning not feeling very rested, but it was Sunday so it was time to take the family to church. Now, we were well connected in the church community and felt fairly well loved and accepted by our fellow parishioners. However, on this particular day, I felt like people were somewhat rude to me. In fact, I started wondering if I had somehow offended them the previous Sunday. Even the minister, who was usually quite friendly with me, was giving me the cold shoulder. My thoughts went further into the hypothesis that I had done some great offense the previous Sunday. I started wondering if I had accidentally belted out a swear word during one of the hymns and just didn't realize it!

Driving home, I shared my concerns with Marla and found out that people had been rude to her also. As we were both wracking our brains to determine our great offense, we pulled into the garage of our home. When we opened the door, we were hit with the worst skunk stench that you could imagine. It was absolutely horrible.

At that point we realized what had happened. Our house had been sprayed in the middle of the night by a skunk. Since we had slept in it all night, we could not smell it much in the morning. However, the people at church could smell us a mile away!

After a moment of humiliation and embarrassment, we started laughing hysterically. The event was so funny we just had to share it with one of our friends. So I called my friend Jeff, who also attended our church. "Jeff, you won't believe what happened. A skunk sprayed us last night. Did you smell us this morning?" After a few seconds' pause, Jeff, with great relief in his voice, said, "Thank goodness, Tim, my wife has been nagging since church to call you and lovingly confront you about your personal hygiene problem."

Jeff and his wife had noticed the bad smell, but avoided saying anything to us because they didn't want to hurt our feelings. What is the moral of the story? Sometimes it is more loving to tell your friends that they stink!

How it applies

Why didn't anyone tell me that I smelled? I wonder what went through their minds:

"I don't want to hurt his feelings! How do you tell someone he stinks?"

"He might get offended or mad if I tell him he smells."

"Get me out of here! Must...get...scented...candle!"

Whatever they were thinking, none of my friends had the nerve to tell me about the stench. Some conflict cowards are like this. They have fears of hurting someone's feelings or making them mad, so they avoid speaking honestly with them. Other times they start to be honest, but they are overpowered when the other person starts to bully them. We have all been in situations that we would like to do over again. Have you ever allowed yourself the fantasy of mentally reenacting a situation where your actions are more assertive (or aggressive) than they were in reality? You know what I'm referring to—replaying a confrontation in your mind, but in your dream you say all the right things at all the right times and really give the person a piece of your mind. Most conflict cowards have used these fantasies to help themselves feel better after an interaction in which they let someone walk all over them.

From my perspective, there are two main types of assertiveness that conflict cowards struggle with. These are 1) compassionate courage and 2) fighting for fairness.

Compassionate courage

Compassionate courage refers to the willingness and ability to tell someone something they need to hear even if it upsets them or hurts them initially. Conflict cowards can come up with all types of excuses for avoiding this type of conversation, but in truth they are choosing to honor their own comfort rather than be strong enough to be honest with their friend. Those that struggle with showing compassionate courage do not realize a negative comment said with care can be a great blessing to someone. When we fail to give negative feedback to our friends, we are keeping them from growing. Many times, true compassion comes in the form of accepting the uncomfortable task of saying something to someone that he just will not like.

Fighting for fairness

Many conflict cowards have a difficult time standing up for themselves. In fact, many times they say the opposite of what they are really thinking. Some examples of mismatches between what is said and what is thought:

A friend takes two days to call you back on an important question.
    What was said: Oh, it's OK, don't worry about it.
    What was thought: I can't believe you took so long to call me back.

A spouse schedules time with friends on a night that the two of you had planned to go out.
    What was said: I can see why you would do that.
    What was thought: You always get your way.

A loved one confronts you on something, but you feel like you did nothing wrong.
   What was said: I'm sorry.
   What was thought: I'm not wrong, but I don't want you to keep yelling at me.

There are many reasons why you might not be willing to fight for fairness. Perhaps you don't feel like you deserve to be treated better. Or maybe you are afraid of the other person's reaction. Sometimes you may feel guilty for asking for what you want. For whatever reason, failing to fight for fairness can lead to bitterness and even depression.

The best response

So what is an assertive response? To understand this we need to look at the differences between a passive, an aggressive, and an assertive response.

How the other person will react to you is highly correlated with which of the responses you choose to show. One way to judge which response you are giving is to assess your response on the following six continuums:

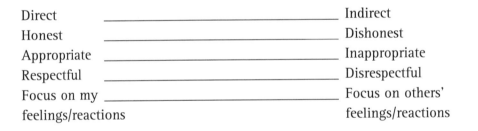

Direct		Indirect
Honest		Dishonest
Appropriate		Inappropriate
Respectful		Disrespectful
Focus on my		Focus on others'
feelings/reactions		feelings/reactions

The direct continuum refers to how much your discussion is to the point and conducted with the right person. The honest continuum reflects how much the discussion truly represents your opinion, thought, feeling, or request. The appropriate continuum concerns the time and place of the discussion (are you bringing up the issue in the right environment and at the right time?). The respectful continuum indicates how well you show honor to the other person's rights in the way that you express yourself to him. Finally, the focus continuum demonstrates whose feelings and reactions are considered most important.

The passive response

Direct	_____	X__	Indirect
Honest	_____	X__	Dishonest
Appropriate	__X_____		Inappropriate
Respectful	__X_____		Disrespectful
Focus on my	_____	X__	Focus on others'
feelings/reactions			feelings/reactions

A passive response is appropriate and respectful, which is positive. However, it is also usually indirect and dishonest. When people give passive responses, they are not direct or they do not share their opinion with the right person. On some occasions, they even say the opposite of what they are thinking to the person with whom they are upset. Passive people tend to focus on the other person's feelings and/or possible reactions rather than their own.

The aggressive response

Direct	__X_____		Indirect
Honest	__X_____		Dishonest
Appropriate	_____	X__	Inappropriate
Respectful	_____	X__	Disrespectful
Focus on my	__X_____		Focus on others'
feelings/reactions			feelings/reactions

The aggressive response flips these continuums. It is positive in terms of being direct and honest, but is done at inappropriate times or is disrespectful in terms of how it is expressed. The focus of attention is on his own feelings and reactions rather than taking into account how the other person might feel or react.

The assertive response

Direct	__X_____		Indirect
Honest	__X_____		Dishonest

Appropriate __X_____ Inappropriate

Respectful __X_____ Disrespectful

Focus on my _____X_____ Focus on others'

Feelings/reactions   feelings/reactions

The assertive response it the best response because it is direct, given to the right person, honest in delivery, done at the appropriate place and time, and is presented to the person respectfully. In an assertive response there is a balance between your needs and the needs of the other person. Both sets of needs are valued and respected.

Obviously, there are varying degrees of expression on each of these continuums, but by realizing where we are behaving on the continuums, we can gain more insight into our style for handling conflict.

There are several steps in an assertive response. The following are adapted from *The Anxiety and Phobia Workbook* by Edmund J. Bourne, Ph.D.

- Evaluate your rights and the rights of the others involved in the situation. What rights do you have to how you feel, think, or behave? What rights does the other person have? What is fair? One way to help determine fairness is to ask yourself, "What rights would I give a good friend of mine in exactly the same situation?"

- If assertiveness is not needed immediately, then set a time to discuss the problem with the other person involved. Pick a time and place that is not threatening or embarrassing to either one of you.

- Communicate the problem situation in terms of the consequences that it has for you. Respectfully let the other person know what impact their behavior has on you. For example, "When you are late to meetings, we do not get as much done as we could if you were on time."

- Express your feelings in "I" rather than "you" messages. For example, "I feel frustrated and perceive that you don't value my time when you are late to meetings," instead of, "You make me frustrated and show disrespect for my time when you are late to meetings."

- Make your request. Directly and respectfully let the other person know what you want. Make it a request and not a demand, when possible.

- When necessary, state the consequences you are willing to implement given the other person's response to your request. If making a request alone does not generate the response that you are looking for from the other person, you can name a positive or negative consequence. An example of a positive consequence would be, "If you eat your vegetables, then you will get a dessert." An example of a negative consequence would be, "If you don't eat your vegetables, then you are going up to your room for a twenty-minute time-out." Of course, this example is for a parent and a child, and I advise you not to threaten anyone with a time-out at work (although some deserve it).

The aggressive person often does a combination of the following:

- Evaluates only his rights.
- Brings up the issue immediately or at embarrassing moments.
- Communicates the message in an attacking or emotional way.
- Blames by using "you" messages.
- Demands rather than requests.
- States negative consequences immediately and as threats.

As you can imagine, the assertive response is more likely to produce a positive response and the aggressive response is very likely to create a defensive response.

One final note about assertiveness. In some cases the other person will argue with you or try to distract you from your request by bringing up other issues. One approach that I have found particularly useful is the "broken record" technique. Using the "broken record" strategy, you simply keep repeating your request until the person responds. Take the following example of someone trying to return a defective item to a store:

CUSTOMER: I found out that this bathing suit has a stain on it and I want to return it.

STORE CLERK: Our policy is not to take returns on bathing suits.

CUSTOMER: I understand that this is your policy, but I am a loyal customer and I want a refund for this purchase because it is defective.

STORE CLERK: You see, people could try these on at home and that is why we just can't refund your money.

CUSTOMER: I understand that this is your policy, but I am a loyal customer and I want a refund for this purchase because it is defective.

STORE CLERK: Did you notice the stain when you bought it?

CUSTOMER: No, and I want a refund for this purchase because it is defective.

STORE CLERK: We really can't do that. If we did it for you, then we would have to do it for everyone. And we can't just change our whole policy.

CUSTOMER: I understand, but I want a refund for this purchase because it is defective.

STORE CLERK: OK, but I'll only make this exception once.

Most conflict cowards make the mistake of either giving up at the first signs of resistance, or they allow themselves to become distracted by the person's comments. The broken record keeps it simple and direct. And if said with a respectful tone and attitude, it can be very effective.

Exercises
Self-reflective exercise: Were you assertive?

Recall three recent times when you had the chance to be passive, aggressive, or assertive. Put an "X" on the continuum representing how direct, honest, appropriate, and respectful you were as well as where your focus was. Be honest with yourself.

Situation #1 (Describe and rate):

Direct	Indirect
Honest	Dishonest
Appropriate	Inappropriate
Respectful	Disrespectful
Focus on my feelings/reactions	Focus on others' feelings/reactions

Situation #2 (Describe and rate):

Direct	Indirect
Honest	Dishonest
Appropriate	Inappropriate
Respectful	Disrespectful
Focus on my feelings/reactions	Focus on others' feelings/reactions

Situation #3 (Describe and rate):

Direct	_____	Indirect
Honest	_____	Dishonest
Appropriate	_____	Inappropriate
Respectful	_____	Disrespectful
Focus on my	_____	Focus on others'
feelings/reactions		feelings/reactions

Examine how you rated yourself on the continuums. Where do you want to change? How can you start that change process?

Practice exercise: Define assertiveness

Using the examples below, create a passive, aggressive, and assertive response for each.

A salesperson comes to your door selling magazine subscriptions. You clearly have a "no soliciting" sign posted on the door.

Passive:

Aggressive:

Assertive:

Your neighbor's dog is frequently free to use your lawn as a bathroom. Your community has clear laws about people using pooper-scoopers that your neighbor seems to ignore.

Passive:

Aggressive:

Assertive:

At a team meeting, one of your fellow team members criticizes you harshly and undeservedly in front of the team.
Passive:

Aggressive:

Assertive:

Your boss asks you to handle a new task force. You are already overwhelmed with your workload and feel unable to take on anything new for several months.
Passive:

Aggressive:

Assertive:

Next steps and additional resources

Practice makes perfect. Go out and practice these assertiveness steps. Initially begin in situations that are less important or crucial to you. Ask a friend to practice with you so that your body language is not threatening, but carries much authority and personal power. Ask your friend to give you feedback on your level of respect shown and confidence demonstrated when giving an assertive response.

For additional assertiveness skills, try *The Gentle Art of Verbal Self-Defense* by Suzette Haden Elgin.

For people that have difficulty saying no, try *When I Say No, I Feel Guilty* by Manuel J. Smith, Ph.D.

"Therefore, each of you must put off falsehood and speak
truthfully to his neighbor, for we are all members of one body."
—Ephesians 4:25

"You may have to fight a battle more than once to win it."
—Margaret Thatcher

"Honest disagreement is often a good sign of progress."
—Mahatma Gandhi

"Words have the power to both destroy and heal.
When words are both true and kind, they can change our world."
—Buddha

"To know what is right and not do it is the worst cowardice."
—Confucius

Chapter 21:

Avoiding the Top Ten Mistakes Made When Dealing with Upset People

Unfortunately, when conflict cowards finally choose to confront bullies, they often do it in a way that is not effective and may actually worsen the problem. In previous chapters we have explored ways to confront others. Here we will look at the top ten mistakes made when dealing with upset people, and we'll use these mistakes to form a strategy to help diffuse the upset person.

Real life

The tension was thick in the room, and we were all waiting for the yelling match to begin. They had just cancelled the flight of a plane which had been delayed three times. The man at the counter was large, sweaty, and not in the mood to accept that his flight had just been cancelled. The conversation went something like this:

> UPSET MAN: *This is unacceptable. I have to get to Houston tonight.*

> AIRLINE REPRESENTATIVE: We don't have any flights going out tonight, and neither do the other airlines. I can get you on a flight in the morning.

> UPSET MAN: *Look! I have been waiting here for hours and I will not accept this lack of professionalism.*

AIRLINE REPRESENTATIVE: Sir, the cancellation is due to weather. There are no other flights going out tonight.

UPSET MAN: *What kind of outfit are you all running? Why couldn't you have told me an hour ago that we were not going to make this flight?*

AIRLINE REPRESENTATIVE: As much as we would love to be psychics and predict as well as control the weather, we can't. I can get you on a flight tomorrow morning.

UPSET MAN: *I have something I have to go to tonight, I can't wait until the morning.*

AIRLINES REPRESENTATIVE: Sir, there is nothing I can do to help you tonight. It's not my fault that we have a blizzard.

UPSET MAN: *This is unbelievable. Simply unbelievable. You can bet that the airline is going to hear from me.*

AIRLINE REPRESENTATIVE: This is our customer service number. Feel free to call them. Now, do you want me to get you on a flight tomorrow?

UPSET MAN: *Fine.*

Airline representative: Fine.

How it applies

A conflict coward by nature, I intensely dislike dealing with upset and aggressive individuals. I think that I would rather trudge fifteen miles through a blizzard, carrying a one hundred-pound backpack, to meet a dentist for a root canal than deal with some of the people I have had to deal with. I hate it, hate it, hate it. But...I do it.

As I mentioned in a previous chapter, I was the target of many bullies growing up. I had a sensitive spirit, was often a teacher's pet, and was carrying around the burden of my parents' divorce. You might as well have painted a red target on my back and sent me out to a firing range. In high school I allowed bullies to intimidate me, tease me, and humiliate me without ever protecting myself.

When we allow bullies to push us around, we can experience many negative effects including:

- Decreased confidence
- A wounded spirit
- Increased health issues
- Emotional exhaustion
- Displacing of anger onto people we love

We may walk around carrying all of the bully's negative energy while he feels better because he was able to vent and now feels powerful and in control.

So, what should you do on those occasions where your goal is not necessarily to build a relationship with people, but rather to diffuse their anger? We will look at what to do by first exploring ten things NOT to do with upset individuals.

Defensiveness (reacting)

It is very common to become defensive and react with anger when dealing with an upset person. After all, they were the one's who caused the problem—right? When we react, we "take on" the emotions of the upset person and vent them right back at her. Unfortunately, reacting causes the one injury that only we can inflict on ourselves; the damage to one's integrity. Reacting gives the other person the power over how you are going to behave instead of maintaining your own identity. Reacting is also likely to escalate the battle rather than diffuse or lessen it.

Pacifying

As presented in chapter 14, some people react to criticism not with anger, but with pacifying and submissive behavior. This type of behavior is often a sub-conscious attempt to get the other person to calm down instead of offering a true apology. Pacifying behavior often has the paradoxical effect of escalating the anger of the upset person. Upset individuals respond much better to genuine and respectful apologies (if applicable) given from a position of strength instead of weakness. If an apology is not called for, then upset individuals likely will be encouraged by an apology and they will continue to badger people until they "win." You are actually reinforcing their bullying behavior by rewarding them with a sense of false power.

Lack of pacing

Many times our first response to an upset individual is to quiet our voice and stay calm. Does this really calm the other person down? In most cases it does not have a calming impact because the person feels like you don't understand how upsetting the situation is to him. A better approach is to match the intensity (voice volume, voice rate, etc.) of the conversation without verbally attacking, and then slowly soften your voice. If you can match his intensity without matching aggressiveness, you often will increase your ability to slowly diffuse the upset person.

Forgetting that understanding is not the same thing as agreeing

How much of your listening time is spent internally disagreeing with what someone is saying versus making sure you understand them? In conflict situations, most people put understanding what the person is feeling at a much lower priority. Attention goes immediately to disagreements. In our minds we start building our argument against what the person said even while they continue to talk. Ideally you should not worry about agreeing or disagreeing until you have made sure that you completely understand what the upset person is saying. If you are not sure, then ask! In fact, keep asking until you are sure you understand.

Verbal and nonverbal behaviors do not match

Has anyone ever told you that he was sorry, but with teeth clenched, arms crossed, and a rigid body posture? Which message did you believe; his words or his body language? We tend to trust the nonverbal messages that we get much more than what the person is saying. Of course, when you give an upset person double messages, he will likely believe the most negative message and could become more upset because he feels you are being dishonest. This only escalates the situation. Whenever my wife and I experience dual messages with each other, we simply ask the other person to give us *one* message instead of two. One message we can deal with. Two or more messages create chaos and mistrust.

Failing to use the appropriate listening style

As presented in chapter 13, there are several ways to listen to others. These are appreciative (listening for enjoyment), empathic (listening in order to emotionally support the speaker), comprehensive (listening in order to organize the information), discerning (listening to gather all the information), and evaluative (listening in order to make a decision). You may be sincerely trying to calm the upset individual, but if you are using the wrong listening style, your responses likely will frustrate them.

Focusing on the details of the discussions instead of the core problem

Excellent communicators do not allow themselves to get sidetracked by insignificant details of the discussion. They:

- Stay with the core issues
- Try to own where they have made mistakes
- Attempt to move toward a compromise

When two people are arguing, they can often bring up additional issues from the past. The argument starts taking all sorts of twists and turns as each individual brings up a grocery list of side issues. When dealing with an upset person, it is important to keep on track with the main issue. If you focus on details and miss the person's main complaint, then the argument will escalate rather than diminish.

Failing to reflect back what the person is saying

If the upset person isn't sure that you have heard exactly what the problem is, he will keep telling you. Reflecting back gives him the peace of mind that you know what he is saying. Think of the purpose that a mirror serves for you. It reflects the image you are projecting—the information and sense of the external you is mirrored back to you. In a conversation, reflecting back can take many forms. Mainly it is important to reflect back that you realize that the person is upset and you are able to and summarize his perspective on what is upsetting to him. If you fail to reflect back their feelings, most upset people automatically will assume you do not understand what they are saying or feeling, and then they will escalate the discussion until you do!

Not utilizing the "100 + 1 percent principle"

Usually our response to an angry person focuses on where we disagree. After we hear what the other person has to say, most of us come back with a different perspective and opinion. We tend to automatically focus on the part of the argument with which we vehemently disagree. Years ago, I heard psychologist Dr. Donald Moine talk about something called the "100 + 1 percent principle." Using the "100 + 1 percent principle" means that you find the 1 percent in the upset person's argument that you agree with and agree with it 100 percent. In other words, in your head you may completely disagree with 99 percent of what the upset person just said. Your natural tendency will be to verbalize this disagreement. However, the wise individual holds his tongue and first talks about the 1 percent of the person's statement that *does* make sense. This 1 percent agreement must be true and genuine, or the upset person might see through it and become more upset. When you agree with the 1 percent, it is important to show that you agree with it 100 percent (or intensely). It will not work to simply throw out a brief pacifying statement of agreement and then spend ten minutes enthusiastically disagreeing with the rest of what she said. Therefore, if your goal is to increase the person's anger, then immediately jump to the point of disagreement. If you want to diffuse them to a more reasonable state of mind, find the 1 percent, that you agree with and agree with it 100 percent.

Putting your "but" in the wrong place

Related to agreeing briefly and then disagreeing intensely is the unwise use of a powerful little word—"but." The word "but" is a powerhouse. "But" is the eraser on a pencil or the control-alt-delete function on a computer. "But" erases everything that came before it. People tend to focus on or believe what they hear after the "but" rather than what comes before it.

Compare these two apologies:

> "It was wrong of me to get so angry, but your behavior really frustrated me."

OR

> "Your behavior really frustrated me, but it was wrong of me to get so angry."

The word "but" erases everything that came before it! If both messages are important to you, and your goal is to diffuse the upset person, then put the agreement statement after the "but," not before it. Even more powerful is to combine it with the 100 + 1 percent principle by agreeing first, then stating the disagreement, and end with "but" and the point of agreement. Reversing the "but" is a simple technique that can save you lots of time and wasted energy.

Thirteen Steps for Dealing with Upset or Difficult People

If an upset person approaches you and your goal is to diffuse their anger, then try the first ten steps:

Step 1: Quickly use the self-talk strategies presented in earlier chapters to calm and control your own reaction.

Step 2: Catch your thinking. Are you trying to understand what the person is saying, or are you building your case against the person? Focus on trying to understand.

Step 3: Check your energy level. Are you shutting down emotionally, or are you carefully matching the intensity without matching the aggression? Try to respectfully match the intensity and slowly decrease it.

Step 4: Make sure you are showing self-respect and confidence in the way you communicate. Do not pacify.

Step 5: Check to make sure that your verbal and nonverbal behaviors are consistent with each other.

Step 6: Listen in the way the other person wants you to hear.

Step 7: Hold your tongue when tempted to follow insignificant details. Keep your mind on the main issues.

Step 8: Reflect back feelings (verbal/nonverbal), so they know you are listening. For example, "It sounds like you are really bothered (upset, angry, disappointed, etc.) right now." Summarize the content of the message (even if you don't agree with it). For example, "If I understand you correctly, your main concern is that you feel like I interrupted you in the meeting."

Check your reflection and summary; if wrong, ask clarifying questions.

Step 9: Use the "100 + 1 percent principle."

Step 10: Get your "but" in the right place.

If you just want to diffuse the person, you can likely stop with the first ten steps. If you want to share your own feelings or work on a compromise, then add the following additional steps:

Step 11: Share your feelings and thoughts. Own them. For example, "I feel (name emotion) when (name behavior)."

Step 12: Return to the person's feelings and the point of agreement.

Step 13: Discuss the next step (i.e., forming a compromise, an apology, etc.).

While there are no magical steps to guarantee that you will diffuse the situation, these techniques will greatly increase your chances of having a more reasonable discussion.

Special steps for dealing with destructive and unresponsive individuals

The book that you hold in your hand is meant for use with most reasonable conflicts. However, there are special cases where the conflict is extreme. At times it is not wise to try to reason with a destructive individuals. In *The Bully at Work: What You Can Do to Stop the Hurt and Reclaim Your Dignity on the Job*, authors Gary Namie, Ph.D., and Ruth Namie, Ph.D., deftly explore approaches for dealing with true bullies in the workplace. They list ten top tactics for bullies:

Top Ten Bullying Tactics
- Blame for "errors"
- Unreasonable job demands
- Criticism of ability
- Inconsistent compliance with rules
- Threats to job security
- Insults and put-downs
- Discounting/denial of accomplishments
- Exclusion, "icing out"
- Yelling, screaming
- Stealing credit

Gary and Ruth Namie are the president and CEO of the Campaign Against Workplace Bullying (www.bullybusters.org). Their book and website are excellent resources for dealing with true bullies in the workplace when the goal is less about diffusing them and more about confronting them. In fact, they list these eight practical steps for toppling bullies:

1) Solicit support from and family and friends.
2) Consult an outside physician or therapist.
3) Solicit witness statements.
4) Confront the bully.
5) File the internal complaint.
6) Prepare the case against the bully. (They present many practical ways to do this, such as searching for code violations,

identifying allies, documenting, and making a liability-focused case.)

7) Present your case to someone two or more levels above the bully.

8) When management responds irresponsibly, take your case public.

While most conflict cowards will likely cringe at the thought of some of these steps, the Namie's research shows that 75 percent of targets end bullying by leaving their job. I find that figure very sad, and I hope that some of us have the courage to help change a system that would allow a bully to gain new targets without ever experiencing her own consequences.

Exercises
Self-reflection exercise: Track your mistakes
Spend some time analyzing which of the top ten mistakes challenge you the most. Over the next several days, put a check mark every time you make one of the following mistakes:

	Put a check mark each time you do one of these
Reacting to the other person's emotions	
Focusing on whether or not you agree with what they are saying before fully understanding them	
Failing to pace their intensity	

Pacifying	
Failing to have verbal and nonverbal behaviors that are consistent with each other	
Failing to listen in the way they want you to hear them	
Getting distracted by details and losing the main issue	
Failing to reflect back the other person's feelings and perspectives	
Failing to use the 100 + 1 percent principle	
Putting your "but" in the wrong place	

Practice exercise: Rewrite the script

Take these various statements that were made by the impatient airline customer and write a response that demonstrates the principles listed.

UPSET MAN: *This is unacceptable. I have to get to Houston tonight.*

AIRLINE REPRESENTATIVE: We don't have any flights going out tonight, and neither do the other airlines. I can get you on a flight tomorrow morning.

Create a reflection response that shows that you understand the man's likely emotions and statement:

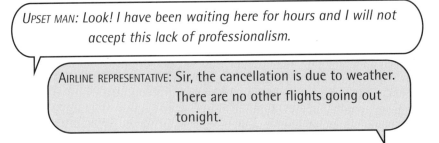

UPSET MAN: *Look! I have been waiting here for hours and I will not accept this lack of professionalism.*

AIRLINE REPRESENTATIVE: Sir, the cancellation is due to weather. There are no other flights going out tonight.

Create a response that would show a negative reaction and focus on a detail:

Now create a 100 + 1 percent response:

UPSET MAN: *What kind of outfit are you all running? Why couldn't you have told me an hour ago that we were not going to make this flight?*

AIRLINE REPRESENTATIVE: As much as we would love to be psychics and predict as well as control the weather, we can't. I can get you on a flight tomorrow morning.

Write a response that indicates that you are using the wrong listening style:

Write a response that shows the right listening style:

> UPSET MAN: *I have something I have to go to tonight, I can't wait until the morning.*

> AIRLINES REPRESENTATIVE: Sir, there is nothing I can do to help you tonight. It's not my fault that we have a blizzard.

Write a response with your "but" in the wrong place:

Write a response with your "but" in the right place:

> UPSET MAN: *This is unbelievable. Simply unbelievable. You can bet that the airline is going to hear from me.*

> AIRLINE REPRESENTATIVE: This is our customer service number. Feel free to call them. Now do you want me to get you on a flight tomorrow?

Write a pacifying response:

Write a respectful, empathic, and confident response:

For an example of each of these, see the appendix.

Next steps and additional resources

Dealing with someone who is upset is not as easy as this chapter may make it sound. It takes great self-control and wisdom. Therefore, ask a friend to role-play with you. Practice the techniques with him or her first. Make sure they make it challenging for you as you walk through each of the steps. Pay special attention to the 100 + 1 percent principle and practice it with them by having them take ludicrous stands on sensitive issues. Ask your friend to go on a tirade about some issue, saying things that they know you disagree with intensely. Try to find the 1 percent you can genuinely agree with completely.

For more on dealing with workplace bullies, try *The Bully at Work: What You Can Do to Stop the Hurt and Reclaim Your Dignity On the Job* by Gary Namie, Ph.D., and Ruth Namie, Ph.D. You can also try *The Complete Idiot's Guide to Getting Along with Difficult People* by Brandon Toropov.

"The greatest danger a target faces in the working world is to have loose or nonexistent boundaries. That person becomes an unprotected target for all who love to hurt others."
—Gary Namie, Ph.D., and Ruth Namie, Ph.D.,
The Bully at Work

"If you want to gather honey, don't kick over the beehive."
—Dale Carnegie

Chapter 22:

Talking About How You Are Talking

Many conversations and arguments that we have can go around in circles. The conversation can take so many twists and turns that you often forget what started the argument! Taking all of these turns in the road of the conversation can limit your ability to ever arrive at the destination of resolving the conflict. One tool that is incredibly helpful in avoiding these pitfalls is the ability to talk about *how* you are talking. In this chapter I will demonstrate the difference between a content response and a global response and examine the impact of using each of these.

Real life

Todd was having second thoughts as he was considering talking to his mother. He was a young and successful businessman who had no trouble managing a team of high performers. However, when it came to handling a visit from his mother, he became a little boy again. Todd had recently gained insight into an issue from his childhood that had continuing effects on him as an adult. His mother's favorite description of Todd growing up was, "He has never, ever disappointed me." She said this statement to Todd and to others around him all of his life (including his siblings, who did not appreciate the statement very much, considering that at times it was connected with, "I wish I could say that about my other children"). Todd had been his mother's pet child, and it was a role that had been both a blessing and a curse. On one hand, he loved the special attention. On the other, he felt tremendous pressure that he could never disappoint her. Todd's mother tended to use guilt as a motivating force to get her children to behave, and Todd's method of avoiding the guilt trips as a child was to always comply with what she wanted.

Unfortunately, his mother's methods never changed, and her description of him continued as he grew to adulthood. At any family gatherings, it was traditional for her to slip "he has never disappointed me" into the conversation in some strange way. She also said it directly to Todd whenever she would come and visit him, and he had decided that he wanted to ask her to stop saying this to him and to others.

So the big night arrived. It was the third day of his mother's visit, and Todd was ready to face the issue with her. Sure enough, she found a way to work the statement into the conversation at dinner. Since it was just the two of them eating together, Todd decided to take a chance. The conversation went something like this:

> TODD: *You know Mom, I have been meaning to tell you that although you may feel like you are giving me a compliment when you talk about me never disappointing you, I actually don't feel good when you say it. In fact, I feel pressure that I can never let you down. I take responsibility for the fact that I feel that way, but I would appreciate it if you didn't say that anymore to me or to other members of the family.*

> MOTHER: What are you talking about? I was just giving you a compliment and now you are treating me like I have done something wrong.

> TODD: *I'm not saying that you have done something wrong, Mom. I am just letting you know how I feel when you talk about me never disappointing you. What I hear is that I can never disappoint you, and I don't want that pressure.*

> MOTHER: So, I'm a terrible mother because I compliment you. You children have never respected me. I guess I have

ruined your life all because I thought you were a good child.

TODD: *Mom, you haven't ruined my life, and I have always respected you.*

MOTHER: Well, this certainly doesn't sound like respect. To call me a terrible mother just because I said nice things about you. Some children should be so lucky. Did I ever beat you or leave you home at night abandoned?

TODD: *No, Mom, you took great care of us. I have absolutely no complaints about how you took care of us. You were and are a great mother and I love you dearly.*

MOTHER: This is how you show me love? I come all the way to visit you, I bring you a gift, I cooked you dinner tonight, and this is the thanks I get? Maybe I should just go home.

TODD: *No, Mom, I don't want you to go. Look, I didn't mean to hurt your feelings. You know, I'm not even sure why I said anything. I've just been feeling some stress at work and I'm sorry that I took it out on you. Can you forgive me?*

MOTHER: You do work very hard, and you have always been the responsible one among my children. But you need to watch that you don't let your work change you.

TODD: *Yeah, sometimes the stress just gets to me.*

Inside Todd's only thought was, "Arghhh!"

How it applies

What in the world happened in that discussion between Todd and his mother? Todd's request started as an attempt to get his mother to stop using the "disappointment" statement. However, it soon turned into a frustrating experience with sidetracked conversation and guilt. Finally, Todd simply pacified his mother by backing down and apologizing. Todd was extremely frustrated, and ended up feeling worse than if he had never said anything. The average conflict coward would then think to himself, "See, it just isn't worth it!"

Todd attended one of my conflict courses the day after this event. During a break, he shared the situation with me and asked me if I had any ideas on how to handle his mother. "How committed are you to breaking this legacy?" I asked him. Todd responded, "If I don't break it, then I think that I will be a slave to guilt my entire life." I went on to explain to Todd that if he really wanted to break the cycle, then he had to be willing to give his mother the "gift of disappointment." I challenged him that he seemed to see his mother's manipulation quite well, but I wasn't sure if he fully saw how he was manipulating her. He had manipulated her by his behavior so that she would never be disappointed in him. "Will you allow her to be disappointed in you if that is what she really feels?" I asked. The question took Todd aback. People had always sided with him about putting the full blame on his mother. Don't get me wrong, I do think that his mother was manipulating with guilt in a selfish way. But I did not have his mother in front of me; I had Todd. While we could have complained about his mother all day, I thought it might be more fruitful to look at what *he* could do about this. While empathizing with his struggle (and I truly did), I did not want to support his view of himself as a victim. "OK, if she is disappointed then that is what she feels and it is her right to feel whatever she feels. So how do I do it?" he asked with conviction in his eyes. It was then that I introduced to him the concept of talking about how you are talking, or global communication.

In any conversation there are multiple layers of activity occurring. On the most basic level there is the content of the conversation. The content involves what words are actually being said. When you talk on a content level, you follow the topic of conversation without addressing the style or process of the conversation. A higher level of communication is the ability to talk about the communication. This "global communication" involves the style with which the words are being said (see the chapter on negative communication patterns) or focuses on what is actually going on in the interaction between the two people. In other words, when you get involved in global communication, you focus on the big picture of the conversation rather than the details of the topic being discussed.

If you review Todd's conversation with his mother, you will see that he started off well but quickly moved to staying on the content of the discussion rather than the way they were talking. This was not an effective way to deal with his mother. He kept chasing her content in the conversation until he shifted from talking about how she was hurting him to apologizing for how he was hurting her. Fortunately for Todd, there was a section in the seminar that I was giving on addressing global communication. He and I met after the session for an hour to map out a strategy to use with his mother. Todd agreed to call me with the results of the discussion.

Here is his play-by-play of the discussion that he had the next night with his mother:

> TODD: *Mom, I want to revisit a discussion that we had last night that did not go very well. I was trying to tell you how I felt about something and, from my viewpoint, you misunderstood what I was saying and somehow I ended up feeling guilty about it. The funny thing is that my original statement to you had to do with guilt. I value our relationship so much that, even though it is awkward, I want to try to tell you one more time what I have been feeling. It is as simple as this: when you tell me or other people that I have never disappointed you, I feel pressure that I can never disappoint you. It is just how I feel, and I'm not making any accusations. I'm just asking you not to say that anymore because I feel pressure when you bring it up.*

> MOTHER: I can't believe you are bringing this up again. How does it make me a bad parent that I compliment you?

TODD: I never said that you were a bad parent. I am just letting you know what I feel, and I think that you are viewing it as an attack on you. It is not an attack on you. All I am saying is that what I hear when you say I've never disappointed you is that I can never disappoint you. I don't want that pressure.

MOTHER: So it is all my fault that you feel pressure. I'm this terrible mother who has the nerve to say nice things about her children.

TODD: Mom, look at what is happening as we are trying to talk about this. I'm saying one thing and you seem to be hearing something else. I would really like you to hear what I am saying and not something that I am not saying. What I am saying is that I feel pressure when you talk about me disappointing you and I'm just asking you to stop saying that.

MOTHER: Fine, I'll stop saying that. In fact, maybe I should just stop saying nice things to any of my children since it might be so damaging to them for me to be nice.

TODD: Mother, it is your right to make that decision if you want to, but I still want you to notice what is happening here between us. I'm making a request and I am trying to be very respectful when I make it. However, I am not feeling that same level of respect back from you. I want this to be a good conversation that brings us closer, not one that pulls us apart.

MOTHER: Well if I am being that disrespectful to you then maybe I should go. You obviously don't want me here.

TODD: To have the relationship that I want with you, I have to be able to tell you what I feel. I don't see that as something wrong to

> do, and yet the way that you are responding suggests that I have done something wrong. I do not want you to go, but I respect that you need to make the decision that is right for you. I am not saying you are a bad mother or that I want you to go. If you hear those things then you are saying them to yourself.

> MOTHER: Well, maybe I need to go where I am appreciated more.

> TODD: Mother, I have to admit to you that what you just said tugs at my guilt strings because again I'm hearing that I have done something wrong. I have done nothing wrong, and I hope that you can accept me and love me even when I don't say the things you want to hear. I do not want you to go. I want to end this conversation and then have a nice time with you. But it is your choice of what you decide to hear and what you decide to do.

Todd's internal thought: You can't teach an old dog new tricks, but I don't have to play the old games.

"Dr. Tim, it was great! I didn't fall for any of the tricks, and I felt like I busted out of a cage I have been in for a long time," Todd shared in his exuberance. He learned that there is power in simply talking about the way that you are talking. "It was really hard to let her be disappointed in me, but I found that it really helped just to say what was going on in the communication. She ended up staying, and although I don't think she fully understood what I was feeling, I think she will be very cautious before using the disappointment phrase again."

Talking about the way you are talking is a powerful tool for breaking free of game playing. In Todd's initial conversation he was basically distracted from his initial mission by his mother's guilt messages. The very thing from which he was trying to break free controlled him. In the second round of discussion Todd kept naming what he was experiencing in the conversation. This was probably a shock for his mother, and her natural response was to try to intensify the "game" by loading up more guilt. You will see this quite often when you are trying to break any habit with anyone. When you attempt to change a pattern, the other person will try to get you to go back to the old style of communication. The old way is known and comfortable, even if it is unhealthy, so they are not about to give up without a fight. This is normal and natural and may be done on an unconscious level by the other person. The important thing is to be persistent during this stage.

Unfortunately, this level of communication can be very difficult and almost impossible for some people who think very concretely. Therefore, I have written the following examples to help.

> SARAH: *Where were you last night? I waited for an hour and I'm upset that you never called. I feel really hurt that you never showed up.*

> JANE: You don't have to get so worked up about it. I just got busy. I never really told you that I would show up for sure.

> SARAH: *What do you mean? I told you how important this was to me.*

> JANE: Well, there have been plenty of times that things were important to me and you didn't come through.

Sarah has several options for responding. Below are three sets of examples that demonstrate content and global responses.

Content response #1: When have I not been there for you?

Global response #1: I am just trying to tell you how I feel and it seems like you are more interested in defending yourself than trying to understand how I feel. I'd be glad to talk about times that I have disappointed you after we finish this conversation. Can we talk this through?

Content response #2: I am always there when you need me.

Global response #2: Look, I don't like how this is going. Can we talk about this in a way that works better?

Content response #3: I'm there for you ten times more than you are there for me.

Global response #3: If our friendship is going to work, we have to be able to talk through things like this. Are you willing to try to understand how I feel?

You will probably notice that global communication is somewhat awkward and is not easy. That perception is very true. It is also true that global communication does not guarantee a positive response from the other person. However, it does increase your chances for getting a better response. By naming interaction patterns, you keep yourself from going down false trails in the conversation. Imagine where this conversation could go with Sarah and Jane if there is no global communication. Here is an example using one of the content responses from above:

> SARAH: *Where were you last night? I waited for an hour and I'm upset that you never called. I feel really hurt that you never showed up.*

> JANE: You don't have to get so worked up about it. I just got busy. I never really told you that I would show up for sure.

> SARAH: *What do you mean? I told you how important this was to me.*

> JANE: Well, there have been plenty of times that things were important to me and you didn't come through.

> SARAH: *I am always there when you need me.*

> JANE: Oh, well what about the time when I waited at the theater for a half-hour and you showed up after the movie started?

> SARAH: *I can't believe you. I told you that my sister's car broke down and I had to get her to her class.*

> JANE: Yeah, you always seem to have to do whatever your sister wants you to.

> SARAH: *I do not have to do what she wants. She had a final that night and she had no other way to get there.*

> JANE: No other way? She couldn't call a friend or her boyfriend?

> SARAH: *She tried calling others and there was no one around to help her. What was I supposed to do?*

This conversation may appear ridiculous and contrived, but it is based on real conversations. Next time you get into an argument and it ends on a completely different topic, you probably were stuck at a content discussion rather than a global discussion.

Now imagine how this conversation would have gone if one of our global responses were put in at any point. Likely, the conversation would have turned into a more productive conversation or the conversation would have ended. Either would have been better than the conversation that ended with her having to defend herself to Jane.

Global communication is hard and does briefly intensify the communication. However, it helps to break patterns of communication that can drain you and beat you up. It is a powerful tool in your communication toolbelt.

Exercises
Self-reflection exercise: Giving a content response

Read the following text in order to determine a content response and a global response.

> JERRY: I thought you were going to get me information on that new prospect by Wednesday.

> MATT: It wasn't my fault. I was on the road all day and couldn't get the information until I got in the office this morning.

> JERRY: I thought I told you how important this prospect was. He wanted a proposal by noon today. Couldn't you have called my assistant and told her to get the information from your office?

> MATT: I was busy with other things. Besides I know this prospect, he doesn't really need the proposal by noon today. Just tell him we were waiting for research from the lab.

Jerry's possible content response:

Jerry's possible global response:

Self-reflection exercise: Reliving a bad argument

Pick an argument that you remember well from the past that went poorly. Try to figure out what was going on in the conversation. What was the core issue getting in the way of you communicating about the topic in question? Record below three global responses that you could have used that might have changed the course of the conversation.

Next steps and additional resources

The next time you feel a conversation going poorly, step back and try to figure out what is going on in the discussion. Try using a global response to get the conversation on a positive track. If you are not sure what is going on in the conversation, simply say, "I'm feeling tension in our discussion and it is important to me that this conversation goes better. What do you think is happening between us?" If the person is not receptive, gracefully drop the conversation. Try to find someone who is receptive in your initial stages of practicing global communication.

For additional techniques to clarify conversations, try *The Clarity Factor: The Four Secrets to Being Clearly Understood* by Ray DiZazzo.

"It must be a peace without victory...
Only a peace between equals can last."
—Woodrow Wilson

Chapter 23:

The Lesson of the Swaying Trees: Embracing Conflict

Sometimes the intensity of our fear is bigger than we are. In these cases no quick technique or approach is going to solve our dilemma. In these circumstances we have to change our entire approach to the conflict. In this chapter we will look at how to handle fear of conflict when it is just too big for any other approach.

Real life

Part of my own journey of self-exploration and awareness came in the form of those drum-beating, woods-exploring, tear-inducing men's retreats that were especially popular in the early 1990s. This was my second experience like this, and the first was so rewarding for me that I was quite excited at what I would discover the second time (can anyone say, "Be careful what you wish for"?). One of the unique aspects of this particular retreat was that a Native American was leading it. Given that I am one-sixteenth Cherokee myself, I thought that this experience would be especially interesting.

On the first night of the retreat, the leaders were talking about doing a "sweat lodge." Now mind you, I had absolutely no idea what a sweat lodge was, but I figured immediately that it had something to do with being hot and sweaty (an understatement for sure) and was probably similar to going into a sauna. So it sounded like it was probably going to be a relaxing experience (readers who have been in a sweat lodge are probably laughing at this point). They wouldn't tell us much about the sweat lodge or even reveal much of the purpose, but they seemed genuinely excited about it and so I was game...until we started walking up to the tepee. At this point I realized that maybe this wasn't going to be the walk in the park I thought it would be.

You see, a sweat lodge is not like a sauna. A sweat lodge is a small confined tepee with layers and layers of skins or burlap bags piled on it so it seems airtight, except for a small flap that serves as the entrance. In our particular sweat lodge, we had room for about eleven men. Therefore, they put in about fifteen. Some of the men wore their regular clothing, some wore towels, and some wore nothing but a (fleeting) smile. Now personally, my idea of a good time is not to be thrust in a nearly airtight tepee structure snuggled up with a lot of hot and smelly men, but hey, when in Rome.... Once the men were gathered in a circle in the tepee, they started bringing in huge rocks that had been cooking in the fire all day. The rocks were glowing red-hot, and they filled the center of the tepee structure with them. As they closed the flap and poured a small amount of water on a few of the rocks, our leader softly started chanting.

I had talked a friend of mine into going to this weekend with me, and he and I were sitting next to each other (almost on each other's lap given the overcrowding situation). We both glanced over with our best "What in the world are we doing here?" looks on our panicked faces. You see, this was a terribly hot summer day, and the rocks had been cooking just a little too long, and we had a few too many people in the tepee and, well, to be honest, I was scared. Scared to death. It was hard to breathe and it was terribly hot, burning hot. After a few minutes, men started covering their faces with their towels and eventually started digging into the dirt to use the mud to cover and cool their bodies. It was hot, it was uncomfortable, and it was frightening on many levels.

One fear was of failure. What if I couldn't make it? What if I had to leave? Would I feel shame? I had never been a tough guy, and all of my previous coward, nerd, and frightened inner child voices were speaking loud and clear to me. But then my confident voice jumped in:

"You're a psychologist."

"You know a million techniques for handling fear."

"This is nothing, you can handle it."

"If they can do it, you can do it."

With renewed confidence, I started using all of my powerful psychological training. I started with imagery and positive thoughts:

"I am in Antarctica. I am in an igloo. I am the snow. I am a snowflake in the wind."

Of course, within a few seconds my powerful imagery turned into:

"I am a melting snowflake. I am FREAKING HOT! I can't stand it! This is horrible. What kind of idiot puts himself through something like this?"

OK, so imagery didn't last long. Then I went to progressive muscle relaxation. In PMR you start with your fists, move up your arms, and eventually move down to your toes, tensing and releasing your muscles in order to release tension from your body. I barely got to my shoulders before one of the men in the tepee panicked and had to leave. As he left, I said to myself, "I'm never going to make it." Then, one by one, men were leaving. It was too hot to take. I looked to my friend secretly hoping that he would be so weak that he would need me to drag him out of the heat and, of course, stay out with him to make sure he was OK. Darn the luck, he was still conscious.

I tried a few more techniques and I knew that I wasn't going to be able to tough it out. The heat, the lack of clean air, the fear were all too big for me. I was helpless. I could not defeat them. Then something hit me. I remembered my own advice to highly anxious clients who were dealing with life circumstances that were bigger than they were. At that point, I removed my towel from my face. Then, instead of pushing myself back from the glowing rocks, I moved as close as I could get to them without getting physically burned. Then I started gesturing my hands toward me as if I was inviting the rocks' hot glow (which I was). In my mind I was saying:

"I accept that you are bigger than me."

"I embrace that you are hot."

"I will quit fighting the fact that I am terrified right now."

"I accept, I embrace. I will not fight you."

In that moment something incredible happened. I started laughing. I started laughing and I laughed on and off for the entire three hours that I was in that sweat lodge. It was hot, but that was all that it was; it was hot. When I quit fighting the fact that it was hot, then all it was, was hot. It was not terrifying, it was not horrible, it was not bad; it was simply hot. I was no longer afraid.

The rest of the day was one of the most peaceful days I have ever had in my life, before or since. I had faced my fear. I had realized that the situation was bigger than my ability to handle it, and in my admission of powerlessness I became powerful and free. Even more amazing is the fact that as I recall this experience, as I sit here and write these words, my spirit has calmed down and I feel free at this moment. Powerful and vulnerable at the same time. Content to be just what I am at this moment. That is what embracing those things that terrify us can do for us. Peace is good.

How it applies

Is your fear of conflict bigger than the techniques that we have discussed in this book? Maybe, but that doesn't mean you need to be a victim to your fear. You see, a victim by his nature needs a relationship with an aggressor. Without an aggressor, there can be no victim. As long as you view the conflict or your fear as a bully, as a dangerous force, or as an aggressor, then you can be a victim. However, when you start viewing conflict or your fear as something that "just is," then your relationship with it changes. Because you are no longer trying to change the situation or your fear, then you actually do change how you are relating to it! It is a paradox that is hard to comprehend if you have never gone through it. But it is a paradox that can change your life once you experience it.

Now the more astute of you probably have noticed that the story of the sweat lodge has nothing to do with swaying trees, as the title of the chapter may imply. So how does this all relate to swaying trees? It does because I am a big movie buff and the idea was represented well in a film I saw a few years after my experience in the sweat lodge. There is a scene in the movie *Phenomenon* that has stuck with me to this day. John Travolta played an ordinary mechanic in a small town who was liked by just about everybody. One night he experienced a strange light that pretty much knocked him out. After this experience, the character has strange powers, such as telekinesis and incredible intellect. I'll let you see the movie to learn more about the plot, but I want to talk about one particular scene in the film.

The main character was working out in his garden with a hoe and was obviously distressed. Everything was falling apart for him. His friends didn't understand him anymore. They thought that he was strange, certainly different than he was before. Some of them avoided being around him. Some of them treated him like he was a circus act and wanted him to perform tricks for them. The woman that he adored from a distance was in her own protective shell. She would not let him get close to her. In addition, he was confused and didn't know what was happening to him. He no longer fit in and he knew it. As he ruminated about his situation, he became more and more upset. His hoe kept hitting the dirt with more and more force. Short, terse movements showed his growing frustration and anger. He was being battered by the forces in his life and was desperately trying to fight back.

For some unexplained reason he stopped for a second and looked up at the trees on his property. The wind was blowing hard and furious just like the factors in his life. However, as he watched the branches, he noticed something both simplistic and profound. The branches were swaying with the wind. As the wind blew, the branches would flow with the direction of the wind. They did not fight against the wind, they did not get rigid in the face of the wind's force; they simply swayed back and forth. As this character watched, he slowly started swaying back and forth just like the branches. As he swayed, his whole demeanor shifted. My assumption as I watched this scene was that he embraced what was going on in his life and started to flow with it rather than fight it. He calmed his spirit and was at peace with all the chaos around him. However, he no longer had chaos within himself. He stopped fighting and just accepted.

Now let's bring this discussion away from the silver screen to you and how you can handle conflict and fear. Imagine that you are sensing the beginnings of a potential conflict. Your body starts to tense and you begin to panic. However, you have invested much time and effort into learning new ways to deal with your fear of conflict, so you start utilizing them. On most occasions, that will be enough and you will come through the conflictual situation with flying colors. However, on a rare occasion, your techniques will just not be strong enough to effectively deal with the challenge. No matter what you say to yourself, not matter what you do, you still will be afraid. You will be intensely afraid. At that time, the best thing you can do is to face your fear, look it square in the eyes, and welcome it as something that is not good or bad, but rather just is. The strange thing is that once you accept your fear, then you are not controlled by your fear. Once you embrace the fact that you can't eliminate your fear, you are actually less stressed. The acceptance of the fear invites the fear to flow through you and thus away from you eventually.

So how does this work? Take, for example, a trip to the dentist. You are sitting in the chair waiting for the dentist to begin drilling. In your mind, you already hear the "zzzzzzzz" of the instrument and are imagining the pain you will experience when she starts ripping into your cavity. Now she is coming closer, and the instrument is actually making that blood-curdling noise as she inches closer and closer. "I can live with this cavity!" your mind screams. Your jaw clenches as the drill enters your mouth. You don't want the drill and you don't want the pain. You start hoping that the stress of the event will trigger your previously unknown mutant telekinetic ability to keep objects away from you with just the power of your mind. You sit in agony as the drill starts doing its terrible, yet healing function.

Now think for a second. How did your reaction to the drill impact your experience of it? Did it help you in any way? Could it have hurt you in any way? The sum of your mental energy was spent fighting off the drill. Therefore, your body tensed up, your mind was racing, and you likely increased the pain of the experience because of your tension. Now don't get me wrong. I am not saying that the above experience should have been a fun one and that changing your strategy would make visits to the dentist something to look forward to. Rather I am saying that you have a choice of feeling the pain of the drill, or feeling the pain of the drill in addition to increased fear and a tense body, plus greater physical pain.

What I do when I am under a dentist's drill or am getting a shot or am experiencing the flu is to embrace the pain. I actually invite it in. I know that I am going to experience it anyway, so why fight it? I actually imagine inviting the dentist's drill into the cavity. Thus my jaw is loose, my body is relaxed, and my mind is calm. Then, all that I experience is the pain that I have to experience anyway—just the pain that I cannot control. I do not create any additional pain for myself.

When you fear conflict and you fight that fear, it is like sitting in that dentist's chair waiting for the drill. You start sweating, and panic kicks in as you are trying to find a way to avoid the conflict. So not only do you have to deal with the conflict itself, but now you have created for yourself the need to escape the conflict with all of the confusion, fear, and pain that comes with it. Your mind reels in retreat as you keep thinking of ways to get out of it, begging yourself to be smarter or faster in getting away from the conflict. In contrast, imagine the person who is afraid of conflict who merely embraces the fact that she is afraid of conflict. She feels the same initial fear that you do, but does not feel all of the added confusion and pain that comes from the need to escape from her fear. She embraces her fear and accepts that fear is all it is. Nothing more, nothing less—just fear, and with that she develops a peace and a greater ability to deal with the conflict situation. Not because she is not afraid of it, but rather because she is *only* afraid of it and nothing more.

The paradox that accepting your fear of conflict decreases your fear of conflict is a wonderful experience. Your goal no longer becomes to get around or away from the fear. Your goal shifts to experiencing the fear. No need to run. No need to hide. You just let yourself feel afraid. So for minor fear levels, you can try many of the techniques that I have already presented for you in this book. When it gets bigger than that, then take the towel off of your face, move closer to the fire, and look at your fear and say, "Welcome."

Exercises
Self-reflection exercise: Experience the phenomenon of embracing

There are many ways to practice embracing something you dread (before applying the activity to something as intangible as fear). In the next few weeks or months see if you can try one of these activities:

- If it is really cold outside, instead of running to your car shivering and desperately trying to get it open before you get colder, simple walk outside at your usual pace and make a motion waving the cold toward you. Invite the cold in saying to yourself, "I embrace you as just cold weather and nothing more."
- If you have a dentist appointment, then try the exercise I

spoke about earlier in the chapter. Invite the drill into your mouth instead of fighting the idea of it drilling into you.

- If it is raining and you would usually run to your car, step outside in the rain and look up into the sky and let the rain fall on you.
- Go to an amusement park and go on a ride that you usually wouldn't go on. Embrace the fear as the ride gets going. Tell yourself that it is OK to be afraid and that your fear is part of the entertainment.
- Watch a scary movie on video or DVD. If a scene frightens you, keep replaying it over and over. Study how the director created the fear. Allow yourself to feel the fear, but keep repeating the scene until it no longer frightens you.
- The next time that you go to the doctor and need a shot, don't turn your head away. Look at the doctor stick the needle in your arm and welcome the healing powers of the medicine along with the initial pain.

Find something that you have been avoiding and do it. Keep doing it until you feel your fear diminish.

Next steps and additional resources

This chapter may have been the most difficult to understand in the entire book. If the ideas seem bizarre to you, then reread the chapter. Find a tree somewhere on a windy day (outside your window, in a forest preserve, wherever) and study how the thinner branches of the tree react to the wind. Notice how they do not fight the wind, but rather flow with it. Allow your body to move in sync with the branches. Notice how it feels (even if it feels silly) to move in rhythm with the branches. Try to imagine what the experience would be like for the branch if it tried to fight the wind. Try to apply this wisdom of nature to your own life.

For additional insights into embracing what you can't control, rent the movie *Phenomenon*.

*"I thank God for my handicaps, for through them,
I have found myself, my work, and my God."*

—Helen Keller

Chapter 24:

Putting It All Together: A Step-by-Step Approach for Dealing with Conflict

In this book I have addressed many aspects of dealing with conflict. However, it is not helpful to have a bunch of tools thrown in a pile without a system for picking the best tool for the task. In this chapter we will take all of the tools discussed and arrange their use in a step-by-step methodology for effectively handling conflict. We will look at four stages: making a decision about facing the conflict, preparing for the conflict, dealing with the conflict, and evaluating your learning from the conflict.

Real life

My father and I had a strained relationship growing up. When he and my mother divorced, I was definitely "on her side." I went to live with her, and my relationship with my father continued to be less than ideal. However, as I became older, Dad and I started enjoying a much better relationship. In fact, we were enjoying a great relationship. We shared a love for movies, public speaking, and greasy, unhealthy hot dogs. I felt as though I had become my father's son again and it was wonderful.

My father died in 1987 at the young age of fifty-two. He died of cancer after two terrible years of struggle. I spent many days of those last two years with him. I remember stroking his head at night in the hospital when I could tell that he was tortured by his dreams. I remember wanting so badly to be by his side when he finally passed away. (I was not.) I remember the many hours of talking and sharing our mutual love and respect.

Those last two years were very special to me and they would not have happened if I had been unwilling to face my father on some issues from the past that were harmful. By having some difficult discussions, we were able to form a good relationship, and I could say good-bye to him without harboring anger from the past. The path to healing between us was not easy, but it was worth every effort.

How it applies

My father, like all of us, was a very complex man. As a pastor, he devoted his life to serving God and bringing others to Christ. As a man, he struggled with his own personal demons and temptations. It amazes me to this day how many of his struggles often became mine. I was strongly impacted by his behavior and could not heal the relationship between us without standing up to him. I don't regret confronting him one bit. I only regret the few conversations that I did not have for fear of losing the wonderful relationship we had formed. Fear is powerful. Fear is tricky. Fear has many faces and forms.

Conflict cowards may avoid conflict for many reasons. Sometimes we let our fear dictate our decisions. Other times, we know what we need to do, but not how to do it. At times we completely distort the situation. To really change your conflict coward ways, you have to go after this with desire, knowledge, and persistence. You will need to know how to prepare for the conflict. You will need to know what to do in the conflict. And you must be willing to learn from any conflict you experience, especially those where you feel like you failed.

Some people question if they will ever be able to get over the fear. I think it is a mistake to place "getting over the fear" as one of your top goals in graduating this program. A better goal is to develop the ability to confront conflict *even* when you are afraid. Your fear probably will not decrease dramatically until you gain confidence in your conflict resolution abilities and see that the majority of conflict events will end on a positive note if you follow the guidelines in this book. Although your fear may never go away completely, once you start having a history of positive conflict, your fear certainly will diminish.

Your ability to handle the fear of conflict will potentially play out in all four stages of the conflict. These are:

1. Making a decision about dealing with the conflict
2. Preparing for the conflict
3. Dealing with the conflict
4. Learning from the conflict

First you must decide if you will deal with the conflict. Then, in preparing for the conflict, you will decrease your fear by using techniques that help you enter the disagreement rational and confident. In the actual conflict, your fear will be under control by stubbornly keeping your focus on the techniques we have discussed. After the conflict, you can help decrease your fear by analyzing your reactions and making sure that you learn something that will aid you in the next conflict situation. Leaving the ranks of being a conflict coward requires you to attend to all four stages. Let's address them one at a time as we work out a step-by-step approach for dealing with conflict.

Stage One: Making a decision about facing the conflict

Accept the fact that you are a conflict coward. Realize that it is OK if you are nervous and hesitant to face the situation.

Examine the possible outcomes of choosing each of the seven methods of dealing with the conflict (chapter 2):

- Avoid it
- Give in
- Be passive-aggressive
- Bully the other person
- Compromise
- Problem-solve with the other person
- Honor the other person

Reflect and determine which of the ten fears that cause us to avoid conflict is strongest for you in this situation (chapter 2):

- Harm
- Rejection
- Loss of relationship
- Anger
- Being seen as selfish
- Saying the wrong thing
- Failing
- Hurting someone
- Getting what you want
- Intimacy

Do a pain/pleasure chart to determine if you should face the conflict (chapter 5). Make sure that you are considering the actual benefits of facing the conflict (chapter 9).

Determine if you should face the fear a step at a time or use the "just do it" approach (chapters 6 and 7).

Do an integrity check to make sure that you are making the best decision (chapter 8).

If necessary, take steps to embrace the conflict (chapter 23).

If appropriate, proceed to stage two; preparing for the confrontation.

Stage Two: Preparing for the conflict

Evaluate your rights and the rights of the other person involved. If you do not need to deal with the issue immediately find a time to discuss the problem with the other person involved.

Determine the source of the conflict for you. Was it:

- Just a difference in personality style (chapter 11)?
- Poor listening or listening with the wrong style (chapter 13)?
- The way the two of you were interacting (One of the four negative communication patterns of critical, pacifying, rationalizing, or withdrawing—chapter 14)?
- A focus on positions rather than interests (chapter 15)?
- A misunderstanding or misperception (chapter 17)?

Do a selfishness check on yourself (chapter 16).

Analyze your reaction. What do you feel beneath the anger? Is your main emotion fear, embarrassment, hurt, frustration, or something else (chapter 12)?

How much of your reaction is due to your *interpretation* of what they did versus what they actually did? Use the TruthTalk formula (chapter 18) to assess your reaction.

Did you contribute anything to the problem?

Use TruthTalk to calm your emotions to a rational level (chapter 18).

Set a time and date to speak with the person.

Special note: While you might not always have the luxury of picking the time and place to deal with the conflict, it is wise to try to do this in the initial stages. This stalling technique will give you time to practice all that you have learned in this book and increase your chances of handling the conflict well. If the other person is insistent on dealing with the conflict immediately, simply tell him something like this:

> "It is extremely important to me that I handle with situation between us well. I care about the relationship and do want to work it through with you. However, I just need a little bit of time to get my thoughts together and make sure that I communicate with you in a positive way. How about we set a day and time to revisit the situation?"

When it is not possible to stall the conflict, do your best to do all of the steps quickly in your head. This may sound like an impossible task at first, but the goal is to practice these techniques enough that you grow to the point that this internal process is second nature to you (yes, it will take awhile, but it can happen!).

Stage Three: Dealing with the conflict
➜ When you are the upset person
Start the conversation by owning any contribution that you made to the problem.

If appropriate, share your view of the main source of the conflict.

Use compassionate courage and assertiveness steps (chapter 20).

Communicate the problem situation in terms of the consequences that it has for you.

Express your feelings in "I" rather than "you" messages. Don't blame!

Focus the discussion on the person's behavior. Talk about "what" they did versus "who" they are.

Ask for their perception of the issue and for feedback on anything that you are contributing to the conflict.

When appropriate, separate wants from fairness (chapter 19).

If the conversation starts to deteriorate in any way:

Stop talking about the details of the issue and start talking about how you are talking with each other at that moment (chapter 22).

Stay at this level of communication until you are both calm.

If necessary, ask for a time-out. Make sure you say how important it is for you to resolve the issue, but that you just need some time to make sure you can deal with it in the best way possible.

If you are able to keep discussing the issue and the person is responsive to your perspective:

Make sure you are talking about interests rather than positions (chapter 15).

Collaborate together to list possible solutions (attempt to create the "win-win").

Evaluate the options.

Select an option.

Agree to a future time to assess how agreement is working.

If the person is unresponsive to you:

Make a request that would fix the conflict.

When necessary, state the consequences that you are willing to implement given the other person's response to your request.

Assume the broken record strategy if needed (chapter 20).

Make sure that you maintain your integrity (chapter 19).

→ When someone approaches you with a conflict and you want to work it out with him:

Show respect; allow him to express his feelings and perspective.

Gather information. Clarify the problem (ask who, what, when, where, how). Make sure you are using the correct listening style (chapter 13).

Reflect back (without judgement) what you hear the other person saying to you. See if you can summarize their main concern (chapter 21).

Explore the source of the conflict.

- Just a difference in personality style (chapter 11)?
- Failure to deal with a primary emotion (chapter 12)?
- Previous poor listening or listening with the wrong style (chapter 13)?
- The way the two of you were interacting (One of the four negative communication patterns of critical, pacifying, rationalizing or withdrawing—chapter 14)?
- A focus on positions rather than interests (chapter 15)?
- Were either of you selfish in any way (chapter 16)?
- A misunderstanding or misperception (chapter 17)?

If appropriate, give your side of the issue and make sure you keep your "but" in the right place (chapter 21).

Return to their perspective.

Collaborate together to list possible solutions (attempt to create the "win-win").

Evaluate the options.

Select an option.

Agree to a future time to assess how agreement is working.

➔ When someone approaches you with a conflict and your main goal is to diffuse the situation (use the techniques found in chapter 21):

Use self-talk strategies to calm and control your own reaction (chapters 17 and 18).

Catch your thinking. Focus on trying to understand.

Check your energy level. Try to respectfully match the intensity and slowly decrease it.

Make sure that you are showing self-respect and confidence in the way you communicate with him (do not pacify as shown in chapter 14).

Check to make sure that your verbal and nonverbal behaviors are consistent with each other.

Listen in the way he wants you to hear.

Hold your tongue when tempted to follow insignificant details. Keep your mind on the main issues (chapter 22).

Reflect back feelings (verbal/nonverbal), so he *knows* you are listening. Summarize the content of the message (even if you don't agree with it). Check your reflection and summary; if wrong, ask clarifying questions.

Use the "100 + 1 percent principle."

Watch where you put your "but."

➜ Optional steps depending on the importance of sharing your perspective and working on a compromise:

Share your feelings and thoughts.

Return to the person's feelings and the point of agreement.

Discuss the next step (i.e., forming a compromise, an apology, etc.).

➜ When you are the upset person and you want to work it out inside of you, but can't or don't want to talk with the other person:

It is not always practical or even possible to resolve conflict with another person. Sometimes people will refuse to work it out with you. Other times the individual with whom you had the conflict is deceased. Occasionally, it is just not wise to try to work out differences with the person. When you decide that it is best to work out the conflict internally, the following techniques might be helpful:

Determine the source of the conflict for you (chapters 11–17).

Analyze your reaction using TruthTalk (chapters 17 and 18).

Assess if you can just let go of your issues with the other person or if you need to find a way to vent your frustration.

If venting is needed, pick one of the following techniques (or one of your own that has worked in the past):

Write a letter to him that he never sees. Allow yourself complete freedom to say whatever you want to say even if it is pretty ugly. Your goal is not to hurt anyone, but to make sure that you get the ugliness out of your system.

Work out your emotion through exercise. When running, punching, doing aerobics, etc., just think, "I am releasing anger," or, "I refuse to hold on to this anger!"

Pretend that the person with whom you are angry is sitting in a chair across from you and tell him what you need to say to him.

After a bad interaction with the person (or a memory of the interaction), physically wipe yourself off thinking, "I refuse to carry around this person's garbage or bad energy."

Use relaxation techniques to calm your body and spirit.

If appropriate, choose to forgive the person for the offense and go on with your life. Use prayer to help you focus on the value of forgiveness and grace.

If your frustration, anger, etc., is recurring, once again analyze if you need to talk with the person to resolve it (or someone else if the person with whom you are upset is deceased or refuses to talk with you).

If your emotions continue, consider seeking out a coach or counselor to help you work through the issues.

Stage Four: Learning from the conflict

You will be able to learn something from every conflict you are in. Remember that you will not do this perfectly, especially when you are first starting. Every time that you learn in hindsight, you will be one step closer to becoming a master at handling conflict. Therefore, after a conflict, do the following:

Assess how well you separated talking about wants and fairness (chapter 19).

Assess how well you maintained your integrity in the situation (chapter 19). What could you have done better to show even more integrity?

Walk your mind through the common causes of conflict (chapters 11–17). Did you address the true conflict?

Examine the steps presented earlier in this chapter. Did you skip any steps?

If you avoided the conflict, why did you? Examine the top ten reasons that people avoid conflict found in chapter 3 to help pinpoint your motivations.

Determine if you fell into any of the mistakes listed in chapter 21.

Redo the exercises in any of the chapters demonstrating techniques that you still need growth in.

Remember, be patient and tackle your growth one step at a time. Your old habits will try to grab you and send you backwards. Don't let them! Remember that it is not uncommon to take three steps forward and two backward. As with any initial self-improvement program, remember to focus on your small successes. Most of all, show yourself grace and kindness as you grow to face conflict and improve your confidence in dealing with difficult situations.

Exercises
Self-reflection exercise: Building confidence
Examine a recent conflict. Regardless of the outcome, try to examine what you did *well* in the situation. Write ten positive things that you did in the conflict:

Action exercise: Use the conflict checklist
Use this checklist to examine your behavior in a recent conflict. Mark each action as "did it," "didn't do it," or "not applicable."

Stage one: Make a decision about facing the conflict
Examine the possible outcomes of choosing each of the seven methods of dealing with the conflict (chapter 2).

Did it _____ Didn't do it _____ Not applicable _____

Reflect and determine which of the ten fears that cause us to avoid conflict is strongest for you in this situation (chapter 2).
    Did it _____ Didn't do it _____ Not applicable _____

Do a pain/pleasure chart to determine if you should face the conflict (chapter 5).
    Did it _____ Didn't do it _____ Not applicable _____

Make sure that you are considering the actual benefits of facing the conflict (chapter 9).
    Did it _____ Didn't do it _____ Not applicable _____

Determine if you should face the fear a step at a time or use the "just do it" approach (chapters 6 and 7).
    Did it _____ Didn't do it _____ Not applicable _____

Do an integrity check to make sure you are making the best decision (chapter 8).
    Did it _____ Didn't do it _____ Not Applicable _____

Stage two: Preparing for the conflict

Evaluate your rights and the rights of the other person involved.
    Did it _____ Didn't do it _____ Not applicable _____

If you do not need to deal with the issue immediately, find a time to discuss the problem with the other person involved.
    Did it _____ Didn't do it _____ Not applicable _____

Determine the source of the conflict for you (chapters 11–17).
    Did it _____ Didn't do it _____ Not applicable _____

Do a selfishness check on yourself (chapter 16).
    Did it _____ Didn't do it _____ Not applicable _____

Analyze what do you feel beneath the anger (chapter 12).
     Did it _____ Didn't do it _____ Not applicable _____

Determine how much of your reaction is due to your *interpretation* of what the other person did versus what he actually did (chapter 17).
     Did it _____ Didn't do it _____ Not applicable _____

Determine if you contributed anything to the problem.
     Did it _____ Didn't do it _____ Not Applicable _____

Use TruthTalk to calm your emotions to a rational level (chapter 18).
     Did it _____ Didn't do it _____ Not applicable _____

Set a time and date to speak with the person.
     Did it _____ Didn't do it _____ Not applicable _____

Stage three: Dealing with the conflict

Start the conversation by owning any contribution that you made to the problem.
     Did it _____ Didn't do it _____ Not applicable _____

Share your view of the main source of the conflict.
     Did it _____ Didn't do it _____ Not applicable _____

Communicate the problem situation in terms of the consequences that it has for you.
     Did it _____ Didn't do it _____ Not applicable _____

Express your feelings in "I" rather than "you" messages. Don't blame!
     Did it _____ Didn't do it _____ Not applicable _____

Focus the discussion on the person's behavior versus "who" he is.
     Did it _____ Didn't do it _____ Not applicable _____

Ask for his perception of the issue and for feedback for anything that you are contributing to the conflict.
Did it _____ Didn't do it _____ Not applicable _____

Separate out wants from fairness (chapter 19).
Did it _____ Didn't do it _____ Not applicable _____

If the conversation starts to deteriorate in any way, stop talking about the details of the issue and start talking about how you are talking with each other at that moment (chapter 22).
Did it _____ Didn't do it _____ Not applicable _____

Make sure you are talking about interests rather than positions (chapter 15).
Did it _____ Didn't do it _____ Not applicable _____

Collaborate together to list possible solutions (attempt to create the "win-win").
Did it _____ Didn't do it _____ Not applicable _____

Evaluate the options.
Did it _____ Didn't do it _____ Not applicable _____

Select an option.
Did it _____ Didn't do it _____ Not applicable _____

Agree to a future time to assess how agreement is working.
Did it _____ Didn't do it _____ Not applicable _____

If the person was unresponsive to you, did you:
Make a request that would fix the conflict.
Did it _____ Didn't do it _____ Not applicable _____

When necessary, state the consequences that you are willing to implement given the other person's response to your request.
Did it _____ Didn't do it _____ Not applicable _____

Assume the broken record strategy if needed (chapter 20).
    Did it _____ Didn't do it _____ Not applicable _____

Make sure that you maintain your integrity (chapter 19)
    Did it _____ Didn't do it _____ Not applicable _____

Stage four: Learning from the conflict

Obviously, you are doing this step by completing this checklist. As you look over the checklist, what is your main area for learning? How could you have done better in this interaction? What will you do differently next time?

Next steps and additional resources

You've done it! You have completed the steps necessary to start your path toward becoming a master of conflict. At this point, determine for yourself if you need to reread the book. Use the results of the above checklist to determine which chapters need extra focus and time. Redo any exercises that could help you continue to grow. Find a friend with whom you can be accountable for following through with your commitment to face conflict and improve your relationships.

Assess in your life if there are any words left unsaid to someone you care about and love. Remember that our time on this planet is short, and it is better to bring about peace with others before you or they pass on. Take some time to be honest with yourself and determine if you have any unfinished business with another human being that needs to be resolved.

For an scholarly look at conflict, try *The Handbook of Conflict Resolution: Theory and Practice* edited by Morton Deutsch and Peter T. Coleman.

> *"To be prepared for war is one of the most effectual*
> *means of preserving peace."*
>
> —George Washington

Is It Worth It and Can I Still Be a Coward?

On September 11, 2001, four planes were hijacked in the United States. Two crashed into World Trade Center buildings, one crashed into the Pentagon, and one crashed into the countryside outside of Pittsburgh, Pennsylvania, without hitting any intended target. The nation was in shock. We felt vulnerable, angry, and were in extreme mourning. My friend Steve called me that fateful day. "Tim, do you remember my business partner when I owned my computer business?" he said. I had met his partner a few times, but did not know him well, but I was sensing what was to come next. Steve said, "I just found out that he was on that plane that crashed near Pittsburgh." Steve's pain over the phone brought up tears in me as well. After our shared tears and my genuine condolences, Steve said, "I'm sure that he was part of the reason that the plane never hit its intended target. He was an easy-going guy, except when there was injustice. He was a Godly man who was kind to others. He would not have allowed them to crash that plane into a target that would have killed more people." Steve was convinced that his former partner and friend stood up to the terrorists involved. I questioned in my own mind if Steve was correct, but of course said nothing. Sometimes we need to form such thoughts to get us through tough times. At least this gave Steve some comfort, feeling that there was some purpose in his friend's death.

Within days of the plane crashes, the news came out. Investigators came to realize that there were at least four men who organized a resistance to the hijackers on that Pittsburgh flight. Steve's friend and former business partner was one of those men. His name was Todd Beamer. Todd talked with an operator while the hijacking was going on, told her of the plan to try and stop them, said the Lord's Prayer with her, and then turned to the other men and said, "Let's roll." The operator heard screams, then silence, then screams again, and then the plane crashed into the ground, killing everyone on board, but likely saving hundreds or thousands of lives. Steve was correct. Todd was the type of man who could not let injustice prevail. He was the type of man who did not seek conflict, but could stand up to it. He was the type of man who did the right thing when someone else did the wrong thing. This final incident was not a surprise to Steve; it fit Todd's life. It was part of who he was.

There will be many times in your life and my life that we will decide that conflict is not worth the pain, hassle, or consequence, and we will avoid it. That is OK; we have to make those choices for ourselves. It is your right to choose when facing conflict is right and when avoiding it is the better choice. However, I pray that for all of us, that we will have the character to face conflict when it is "just the right thing to do." Todd's example is unique, and few of us will have to face conflict at that extreme level. However, we are surrounded by minor injustices every day. The coworker who is demeaned by a manager, the child who is shamed by the parent, the spouse who is deeply hurt by the person who is supposed to love him more than anyone else on the planet. I hope our character is the sort that will face these conflicts with wisdom, discipline, and skill. My friend had no evidence that Todd helped stopped those terrorists, but he knew Todd's character so he knew what he did. What would people predict from your character?

What successful people know about conflict is that maintaining your character and integrity are far more important than the outcome of the conflict. This means that sometimes you will fight, sometimes you will step down, and sometimes you will find other solutions. But your behavior will be determined by what you believe is the right thing to do, not by your fear or by the behavior of the other person. You can win an argument and lose something far greater when you betray who you are in conflict. Successful people know that no one can take away "who" they are. You can take away a job, you can take away a relationship, and in extreme cases you can take away a life. You cannot take someone's integrity or character away from him or her. No one has the power to destroy another's character. We only have the power to betray our own. Successful people know this and they protect their character like a watchdog.

As I confessed to you at the beginning of this book, I'm a conflict coward. I hate it and I will always hate it. But I have learned to do it and do it well. I have even learned at times to really appreciate what it can do for me and for others when it is done well. When it is done poorly, we all suffer. As a world, we must learn how to handle our differences. We must learn how to handle our anger. We must learn how to handle our conflict. Our growth, esteem, intimacy, and sometimes even our lives depend on it.

Next steps and additional resources

It is now time to practice, practice, practice. By reading this book, you have learned how to motivate yourself to face conflict and how to actually do it well.

I applaud your courage for working through this book and wish you the very best in your road toward improved communication and conflict confidence.

> *"Man must evolve for all human conflict a method*
> *which rejects revenge, aggression, and retaliation.*
> *The foundation of such a method is love."*
>
> —Martin Luther King Jr.

Appendix

Listening styles
Chapter 13

As Taylor's manager, how would you answer the following questions?

What are the main issues in this situation?

Taylor was only using one listening style with Sue (empathic listening). While empathic listening might have been appropriate in the beginning, it was not motivating Sue to take positive action. The meetings between Sue and Taylor were ineffective because no positive action was encouraged. Taylor may have been able to help Sue more by taking a comprehensive listening approach to help figure out the sources of conflict and evaluative listening to move Sue toward positive action.

What would you do to help Taylor in this situation?

I would coach Taylor on her listening style. I would want to see what type of assumptions she makes about how a manager should handle conflict between individuals she manages. I would coach her to see how her approach was not only upsetting her, but also not helping Sue.

What does Taylor need to do?

In my opinion, Taylor needs to go back to Sue and confess that she did not handle the situation in the best way possible. She needs to point out to Sue that the way they are talking about the conflict is not helping and to motivate Sue to work toward conflict resolution behavior.

Samantha's TruthTalk
Chapter 18

The Catalyst for Your Reaction (What *happened?* Record the facts about the situation that upset you.)	One of Samantha's managers came into her office complaining about one of the other managers.
Mindset (What were you *saying* to yourself that upset you? What core beliefs played a role?)	Samantha thought to herself, "Here we go again. They can't ever resolve these things themselves. If I don't calm the situation down then someone is going to quit."
Feelings (How did you *feel* about the event?)	Samantha felt apprehensive, concerned, and angry.
Behavior (What did you *do* in response to the event?)	Samantha tried to calm the manager down and empathized greatly with his feelings. She then went to the other manager and calmed her down and empathized with her. She asked both of them to let it go and support one another.
Truth Test (Is what you are saying about the event *completely* true?)	*It is very unlikely that her managers never resolve things. Also, she has no proof that this event could lead to anyone quitting. So the answer is no, it is not completely true.*

Strategic Test (Is your response to the event *helping* or hurting you?)	*Samantha's feelings do not help her in this situation, and her approach for dealing with the problem does not truly resolve anything, so her response is* hurting *her, not helping her.*
New Mindset (What is a truthful, but *more helpful* mindset in response to the event?)	*Samantha could say to herself, "No one is talking about quitting. Conflict is perfectly normal in an organization. I want to use this situation to help my managers learn how to work better together and make the team more cohesive."*
The Productive Response (How could you respond to this event in a way that would be even more *productive?*)	*Samantha could pull both managers into her office and facilitate a productive discussion. She could let them know that to be leaders in the company, she needs them to excel at managing differences. She could then work up developmental plans with each of them so that they could learn skills for conflict management.*
The Opportunity Challenge (What are some *positive* results that are possible from this event?)	*This is a chance to help her managers grow to the next level in terms of their ability to deal with conflict. If she can train them (or have them trained) well enough, eventually they could take responsibility to helping others deal with conflict in the company and thus save Samantha time.*

Note: Eventually Samantha discovered that she had a core repeating irrational thought of, "When people disagree, someone leaves." Practicing a more productive thought to replace this one led to great success in confronting conflict in multiple situations.

TruthTalk Thought-Changing Form
Chapter 18

The Catalyst for Your Reaction (What *happened?* Record the facts about the situation that upset you.)	
Mindset (What were you *saying* to yourself that upset you? What core beliefs played a role?)	
Feelings (How did you *feel* about the event?)	
Behavior (What did you *do* in response to the event?)	
Truth Test (Is what you are saying about the event *completely* true?)	

Strategic Test (Is your response to the event *helping* or hurting you?)	
New Mindset (What is a truthful, but *more helpful* mindset in response to the event?)	
The Productive Response (How could you respond to this event in a way that would be even more *productive?*)	
The Opportunity Challenge (What are some *positive* results that are possible from this event?)	

Rewrite the script
Chapter 21

Take these various statements that were made by the impatient airline customer and write a response that demonstrates the principles listed.

UPSET MAN: *This is unacceptable. I have to get to Houston tonight.*

AIRLINE REPRESENTATIVE: We don't have any flights going out tonight and neither do the other airlines. I can get you on a flight tomorrow morning.

Create a reflection response that shows that you understand the man's likely emotions and statement:

> *I hear that you are very frustrated and that it is very important for you to get to Houston tonight.*

> UPSET MAN: Look! I have been waiting here for hours and I will not accept this lack of professionalism.

> AIRLINE REPRESENTATIVE: Sir, the cancellation is due to weather. There are no other flights going out tonight.

Create a response that would show a negative reaction and focus on a detail:

> *How dare you accuse me of being unprofessional! This has to do with weather, not our service. This is just idiotic!*

Now create a 100 + 1 percent response:

Sir, I agree completely with you that you have been waiting a long time and I know it must be extremely frustrating to you to have waited all of this time just to have the flight be canceled.

> UPSET MAN: What kind of outfit are you all running? Why couldn't you have told me an hour ago that we were not going to make this flight?

> AIRLINE REPRESENTATIVE: As much as we would love to be psychics and predict as well as control the weather, we can't. I can get you on a flight tomorrow morning.

Write a response that indicates that you are using the wrong listening style:

> *Well, an hour ago we were trying to determine if your plane had left the Atlanta area yet, as we needed that information to determine the exact time that your flight was going to arrive.*

Write a response that shows the right listening style:

> *I understand completely that it has been frustrating for you that we were not able to give you an update until now. We hate it, too, when we can't get the information that we need to keep our customers from experiencing the kind of frustration that you are going through.*

> UPSET MAN: *I have something I have to go to tonight, I can't wait until the morning.*

> AIRLINES REPRESENTATIVE: Sir, there is nothing I can do to help you tonight. It's not my fault that we have a blizzard.

Write a response with your "but" in the wrong place:

> *I really wish that we could get you where you need to go tonight, but there is no way that we can get you out on a flight tonight.*

Write a response with your "but" in the right place:

> *There is no way that we can get you out on a flight tonight, but I really wish we could get you where you need to go.*

> UPSET MAN: *This is unbelievable. Simply unbelievable. You can bet that the airline is going to hear from me.*

> AIRLINE REPRESENTATIVE: This is our customer service number. Feel free to call them. Now do you want me to get you on a flight tomorrow?

Write a pacifying response:

> *Sir, let me see if I can get you some voucher tickets for all of the trouble that we have put you through.*

Write a respectful, empathic, and confident response:

> *Sir, I feel badly about the frustration you are going through and really wish that we could do something to get you to Houston tonight. I would like nothing more than to do that. However, the safety of our customers is our number one concern and I have been informed that the flight is canceled. If I could help you I really would and I respect whatever you need to write to the airline.*

Bibliography

Alessandra, Tony and Michael O'Connor. *The Platinum Rule*. New York: Warner Books, Inc., 1996.

Bisiker, Richard. *Unlock Your Personal Potential: A Self-Coaching Workbook*. Naperville: Sourcebooks, Inc., 2001.

Bourne, Edmund J. *The Anxiety and Phobia Workbook*. Oakland: New Harbinger Publications, Inc., 1990.

Bradshaw, John. *Healing the Shame that Binds You*. Deerfield Beach: Health Communications, Inc., 1988.

Bradshaw, John. *Homecoming*. New York: Bantam Books, 1992.

Burns, David D. *Ten Days to Self-Esteem*. New York: William Morrow and Company, Inc., 1993.

Coleman, Peter and Morton Deutsch. *The Handbook of Conflict Resolution: Theory and Practice*. California: Jossey-Bass, 2000.

Covey, Stephen. *The 7 Habits of Highly Effective People*. New York: Simon & Schuster, 1989.

Crabb, Larry. *Men and Women: Enjoying the Difference*. Grandville: Zondervan, 1993.

DiZazzo, Ray. *The Clarity Factor: The Four Secrets to Being Clearly Understood*. Naperville: Sourcebooks, Inc., 2000.

Elgin, Suzette Haden. *The Gentle Art of Verbal Self-Defense*. New York: Barnes & Noble Books, 1980.

Ellis, Albert and Robert A. Harper. *A New Guide to Rational Living*. Hollywood: Wilshire Book Company, 1975, 1961.

Fisher, Roger, William Ury, and Bruce Patton. *Getting to Yes: Negotiating*

Agreement Without Giving In. New York: Houghton Mifflin Company, 1981, 1991.

Gray, John. *Men are from Mars, Women are from Venus: A Practical Guide for Improving Communication and Getting What You Want in Your Relationships.* New York: HarperCollins Publishers, Inc., 1992.

Helton, Jeff and Lora. *Authentic Marriages: How to Connect with Other Couples through A Marriage Accountability Group.* Chicago: Moody Press, 1999.

Jeffers, Susan. *Feel the Fear and Do It Anyway.* New York: Fawcett Books, 1992.

Kersey, Cynthia. *Unstoppable: 45 Powerful Stories of Perseverance and Triumph from People Just Like You.* Naperville: Sourcebooks, Inc., 1998.

Lucado, Max. *In the Grip of Grace: You Can't Fall Beyond His Love.* Texas: Word Publishing, 1996.

Marston, William. *Emotions of Normal People.* London: Kegan Paul, Trench, Trubner & Company, 1928.

Namie, Gary and Ruth. *The Bully at Work: What You Can Do to Stop the Hurt and Reclaim Your Dignity on the Job.* Naperville: Sourcebooks, Inc., 2000.

Peck, Scott M. *The Road Less Traveled.* New York: Simon & Schuster, 1978.

—. *Further Along The Road Less Traveled.* New York: Simon & Schuster, 1993.

Ritchy, Tom and Alan Axelrod. *I'm Stuck, You're Stuck: Breakthrough to Better Work Relationships and Results by Discovering Your DISC Behaviorial Style.* San Francisco: Berrret-Koehler Publishers, 2002.

Robbins, Anthony. *Awaken The Giant Within.* New York: Fireside, 2001.

Satir, Virginia. *People Making.* Palo Alto: Science & Behavior, 1972.

Smalley, Gary and John Trent. *Love Is A Decision: Thirteen Proven Principles to Energize Your Marriage and Family.* Texas: Word Publishing, 1989.

Smith, Manuel J. *When I Say No, I Feel Guilty.* New York: Bantam Books, 1978.

Toropov, Brandon. *The Complete Idiot's Guide to Getting Along with Difficult People.* New York: Alpha Books, 1997.

Ursiny, Timothy. *The Coach's Handbook: Exercises for Resolving Conflict in the Workplace.* Wheaton: Advantage Coaching & Training, Inc., 1999.

Weeks, Dudley. *The Eight Essential Steps to Conflict Resolution.* New York: Tarcher-Putnam, 1994.

Weisinger, Hendrie. *Dr. Weisinger's Anger Workout Book.* California: Jossey-Bass, Inc., 1998.

Index

100 + 1 percent principle, 218–19, 226

A
aggression, 169–70, 174, 201, 205, 207, 214–15
anger, 29, 78, 105–11, 175, 252; diffusion, 215–22; irrational thinking, 160, 161
appreciative listening, 116, 118–19
approach, 94
appropriateness, 204
assertiveness, 201–12, 254
avoidance, 7, 13, 19, 25–34, 59, 128, 171–73, 174, 192, 250, 251, 264; pain vs. pleasure, 45–55, 252

B
Beamer, Todd, 263–64
behavior patterns, 89–104
behavior types, 94
body language, 217
Bourne, Edmund J., 206
bullying, 15–16, 20, 202, 215, 221, 251, 264

C
Campaign Against Workplace Bullying, 221
catalysts, 178
change, 35–41, 98, 234
childhood, 174
cognitive therapy, 169
common sense, 155–65
communication, 125–33, 204–9; DISC system, 94; global, 231, 234–36; levels, 189–200, 252; nonverbal, 217; with upset people, 215–22. *See also* sharing
compassionate courage, 203, 254
comprehensive listening, 116, 119–20
compromising, 16–17, 20, 251
confidence, 37–38, 78
conflict, 108, 118; analysis, 257–58, 262; benefits, 75–82; dealing, 253–57, 260–62; decision-making, 251, 258–59; DISC system, 99; embracing, 242–46, 252; fear test, 8–10; preparation, 252–53, 259–60

conscientiousness, 94–99, 101
consequences, 206, 207, 254
cost-benefit analysis, 22
Covey, Stephen, 84
Crabb, Larry, 150
criticism, 126–27, 216

D
defensiveness, 215
depression, 78
disappointment, 230
DISC evaluation, 104
DISC system, 94–96
discerning listening, 116, 120
dominance, 94–97, 101

E
emotions, 94, 179; irrational think-
    ing, 161
empathic listening, 116, 119
evaluative listening, 116–17, 120–21
exercise, 257
exercise (pain vs. pleasure), 47–49
expectations, 175, 184
eye-to-eye communication, 130

F
failure, 30, 175, 252
fairness, 19–93, 197, 198, 203, 206, 254
family influence, 78–80
fear, 27–34, 66, 175, 202, 242–45,
    250–51; confrontation, 57–62,
    63–68; irrational thinking, 159
fear hierarchy, 60, 61

Fisher, Roger, 136
flexibility, 98
focus, 204, 217
focus of attention, 94–95
forgiveness, 194–95, 257
forgiveness, 72

G
giving in, 13–14, 19
global communication, 231, 234–36

H
habits. See behavior patterns
harm, 27–28, 252
honesty, 204
honoring, 18, 21, 251
human resources, 53

I
influence, 94–98, 101
insight, 174–75, 184
integrity, 69–73, 192, 193, 197, 199,
    252, 254, 264
interests, 136–41, 252, 254
intimacy, 32–33, 78, 252
irrational thinking, 155, 157–165,
    169. See also self-talk

L
letter-writing, 256
life balance wheel, 114
listening styles, 113–24, 217, 252. See
    also by specific style
loyalty, 98

M

marriage accountability group, 150
Marston, William, 94
mindset, 178, 181
Moine, Donald, 218
motivation, 84

N

Namie, Gary, 221
Namie, Ruth, 221
negative reinforcement, 59
negativity, 178

P

pacification, 127, 216
pacing, 216
pain vs. pleasure, 47–55, 67; chart, 51
passive resistance, 7
passive response, 205
passive-aggression, 14, 19–20, 251
Patton, Bruce, 136
perception, 47–53, 89, 155, 174, 252
perfectionism, 98
personal goals, 40
Phenomenon (motion picture), 242
positions, 136–141, 252, 254
problem-solving, 17–18, 20–21, 99, 251

R

rationalization, 127–28
reacting. *See* defensiveness
reflecting back, 218, 255
rejection, 28, 252
relationship loss, 28

relaxation, 257
respect, 78, 130, 158–59, 204
role-playing, 226, 257

S

self-care, 148–49, 151
self-respect, 78
self-talk, 161–62, 175–76, 219, 253. *See also* irrational thinking; TruthTalk
selfishness, 29–30, 145–53, 252, 253. *See also* wants
sensitivity, 31
sharing, 192, 196, 198
skills, 84
spousal abuse, 53
steadiness, 94–98, 101
structure, 175, 184
systematic desensitization, 59

T

tenacity, 175, 184
TruthTalk, 160, 161, 169–88, 253, 256; thought changing form, 176–85

U

understanding, 216
Ury, William, 136

V

values, 72. *See also* integrity

W

wants, 189–200, 254
withdrawal, 128

Information about Advantage Coaching & Training

Advantage Coaching & Training works with both individuals and corporations to enhance performance and life satisfaction. We believe that people perform at their best when they can achieve their goals, live their passion, and fulfill their mission. All of our coaches offer a complimentary consultation to anyone seeking to change and grow.

Along with coaching individuals, Advantage Coaching & Training has provided coaching and training to a wide variety of companies both large and small. We help individuals to achieve, achievers to lead, and leaders to live balanced lives. Our services are divided into the three main areas of assessment, training, and coaching.

Assessment Services

Standardized behavioral profiles are an impactful way to learn more about individual strengths and weaknesses. Through profile administration and feedback, individuals can learn how to enhance those strengths, overcome their weaknesses, and relate better to others. We utilize materials from several different companies that provide strategic input on a variety of self-improvement topics including conflict management, leadership, behavioral styles, listening styles, and communication excellence.

Training Services

Advantage Coaching & Training provides workshops to corporations that are relevant, interactive, practical, and customized to ensure maximum impact. Some of our most sought-after presentations are conflict resolution, high performance in time of transition, teambuilding, sales performance, time management, and leadership skills. Advantage Coaching & Training also offers designation courses for individuals who want to coach within or outside of organizations. In addition to workshops and keynote addresses, we also have training products, including workbooks on conflict and videos addressing coaching skills and dealing with difficult people.

Coaching Services

Coaching brings out the very best in people in order to increase productivity and life satisfaction. Coaches at Advantage Coaching & Training work with individuals, teams, and corporations on goals related to life balance, peak performance, relationships, leadership, and other areas. Since many people have not experienced coaching, we offer a complimentary coaching session to help determine possible coaching goals and approaches. From career coaching to life balance to peak performance to working with conflict, we help people excel by aiding them in focus, accountability, and conscious living. Anyone truly interested in trying coaching receives a free initial consultation with one of our coaches. This allows people to try coaching without any pressure or risk. Coaching can be done in person or over the telephone. If you prefer someone in person and we do not have any available coaches in your area, Advantage Coaching & Training will work to find someone locally with whom you can work.

For more information on all of our services or to order products, you can visit Advantage Coaching & Training at www.advantagecoaching.com or contact us at (800) 657-5904.

About the Author

Tim Ursiny, Ph.D., CBC, RCC, is the president and founder of Advantage Coaching & Training. He is an executive coach and trainer specializing in helping executives and their teams reach peak performance in both their professional and personal lives. As a certified business coach, he has trained thousands of professionals at every level of management. His areas of focus include conflict management, dealing with transition, communication skills, team-building, coaching skills, stress management, overcoming blocks to success, and work-life balance.

Dr. Ursiny received his undergraduate degree from Wheaton College and his doctorate in psychology from Northern Illinois University. He is a member of the Worldwide Association of Business Coaches, the International Coach Federation, the Chicago Chapter of the American Society for Training and Development, and is the former chair of corporate coaching for the National Association of Business Coaches.

Dr. Ursiny speaks on a regular basis for Fortune 500 companies wanting workshops that are entertaining yet full of practical substance. Both his coaching and training work are oriented toward practical actions that help people utilize all of their gifts, talents, and abilities.

While oriented toward top performance, he also believes in living a balanced life and spending each day in gratitude. He lives with his loving wife and three sons in Wheaton, Illinois.